Guendalina Salimei

CONTEMPORARY CARAVANSERRAIS
New models for public spaces and city squares

FOREWORD

The publication in English of this text has made it possible to integrate and review some parts of this research and to talk about the choice of its title, a term, *Caravanserai*, which over time has come to signify for the Middle East and in particular for the Islamic world a large container of functions, activities, practices and encounters.

Situated along communication routes to offer a stopoff point for caravans, these places were in simple forms an encounter between the Mediterranean landscape and architecture, an architecture of limits between the pathways which were the fruit of human activity, and boundless nature.

Caravanserais, created to offer refreshment and repose to travelers and merchants, were a true institution in the Islamic world they belong to the memory and the tradition of living, becoming a spatial arrangement for cities and landscapes, a model of organization and control of territories, a "large-scale territorial planning device" that defined the formal characteristics of cities and territories, re-proposing them in 'symbolic form'."[1] They were the most authentic expression of nomadic and semi-nomadic culture, and although almost all are now disused and abandoned, they have greatly influenced the organization of the landscape.

Not all caravanserai resemble each other. They may have different formal features in relation to their function, whether as stopoff points or way stations, or whether placed on trade or information routes. Likewise, the distance between them varies according to the different travelling speeds of caravans as opposed to riders bearing information.

What remains unvaried is the formal matrix of their enclosures, circumscribed perimeters which from Egyptian times to Greek and Roman times transformed their form-function from a defensive one to a generatrix one of a space in itself significant, its central empty space, the agora, and also defined another space, the outer one of the landscape.

It is in this key that the present research intends to use the similarity between distant places, both in time and space, and contemporary buildings, where there is a continuous transposition of themes and meanings between inner and outer, where limits are in themselves meaningful in the panorama of the modern city. I wanted to reflect on the forms and meanings that this particular type of space takes on in the contemporary world.

[1] L. Ficarelli, *I Caravanserragli, Architetture commerciali nei paesaggi mediterranei*, Florence, Aion Edizioni, 2015, p. 35.

Introduction   **pg. 7**
The new squares of today and tomorrow

Cp. 1

pg. 17
Evolution of new spaces

A day-long journey
Play as an experience outside of daily life
Theater as a simulation of reality

Cp. 2

pg. 39
**Evolutions in the ways of living
the aesthetic experience**

Bewilderment and swing
A more sensitive and emotional approach
An experience "truer than the truth itself"

Cp. 3

pg. 61
A city within the city

Beyond all typologies
Acceleration
Narration
A great container
Autonomy of the parts, unity of the "whole"
Inside-outside, private-public
Flexibility and its variations
Nucleus and shell

Cp. 4

pg. 115
Living places living spaces: new hypotheses taking shape

Transforming what exists
Reintroducing archetypes
The great roof
The basement as metaphor of the labyrinth
The bridge-building
The totem-building
The arcade-building

Cp. 5

pg. 189
The characters of a new language coming into being

The façade and its double
Nature and artifice
Heavy and light
The labyrinthine space
...towards a responsible design

Bibliography   **pg. 222**

Le Passage Choiseul, Paris, 1829.

Introduction

The new squares of today and tomorrow

Collective places, because of their distinction of being spaces assigned to carrying out functions of social relationships in the contemporary city, are places that more than any others manifest and reflect social change and seem ideal interpreters of the features, pace and modes of contemporary life.

These places may be shopping malls, airport terminals and railroad stations, convention centers, cultural centers, hotel and office lobbies, gas stations, museums and a thousand more.

Though predominantly empty spaces, today they tend to be great enclaves with large covered spaces and present themselves no longer as representative places, but as 'urban scenes'; often a 'theater' of highly significant events, they are in effect scenic images not so much keen on participating in the surrounding city as to be themselves urban microcosms, small worlds in their own right, alternate ambiences.

Contemporary collective places are undergoing a major transformation, also determined by a different way of experiencing recreational and cultural activities. Having lost their representative function of distinct values, generalizing character and bearer of a single identity, they must, if they are to be utilized in a positive way by the community, interpret society's needs, expressing tension and provoking emotions, and, above all, flexibly serve a variety of uses and meanings even over the course of time.

The sites that effectively interpret what we might call the new centers of the future come to grips in some way with the representative intentions of multiple identities of a population that no longer sees itself as subdivided into social classes but identifies with small groups, tight-knit cliques that become fragmented almost to a single individual.

Unlike the spatial continuity that the traditional squares had with the urban fabric, today's collective places no longer interpret a distinct value, a symbol of something, but are mostly just themselves; in them the eye must no longer grasp the entire space in a single glance but be able to lose itself, to the near brink of disorientation. In this way they can evoke emotions, be places where it is possible to enjoy new, formative and meaningful psychological and physical experiences.

The new centers are gathering places largely characterized by fluid, dynamic spaces that can be utilized and experienced in different ways in different seasons and at different times of day. They are places where the citizen no longer discovers any value, the fundamental certainties of his or her existence, such as those typically expressed by religious buildings, the centers of political and administrative power, traditional markets and museums, but can stroll through and live out emotional experiences, learning to tarry among various possible paths, from those that are familiar to those that offer unexplored sensations.

Collective places, precisely because they are centers of attraction and aggregates of charged energy, can also bring about significant changes in the surroundings, and hence are important opportunities for renewal. It follows that some parts of the city, since they are close to nodes of interchange and thus easily accessible, become, more than others, potential poles of attraction capable of involving people, renewing surrounding areas, pointing to possible solutions, and thus conferring identity on parts of city that had none.

These places have the potential to interepret in a contemporary key the role of the squares of yesterday, to become the new squares of today and tomorrow.

A definition of public space becomes increasingly difficult for critics of

Crystal Palace, J. Paxton, Universal Exposition of London, 1851.

Introduction

architecture, who try to identify an urban order from the coordinates visible between built space and social space, but find only absence, repetition and fragments. For most it is impossible to recognize those 'places' as public spaces. Undoubtedly, if public space is defined in terms of traditional fixed and physical categories of the past, such as the agora, the forum, the square, the street, the new places leave much to be desired, despite a public that constantly flocks to them. However, a more flexible definition will enable us to consider both 'public' and 'space' as concepts continually redefined in reality, and to interpret the existence of these new spaces as proof of the non-disappearance of public space, and the emergence of a new type of not yet fully understood public domain[1].

Allen Lambert Gallery, S. Calatrava, Toronto, 1992.

In a reversal of the traditional logic of architecture, internal spaces become the focal points of buildings, making possible their operation and placement in any context, from urban centers to open countryside. Fredric Jameson explained how these spaces used for public activities are, although sometimes private, a new category of social space, halfway between the private space of domestic life and public, collective spaces characterized by a complex mechanism of exclusion but also by a strong tendency toward inclusion. Allowing access to vast crowds, they have replaced traditional public spaces; airports function as entry points to the city and shopping malls are becoming the closest thing possible to a city square[2]. As never before, in recent years public urban places have been undergoing powerful transformations[3].

What are these places, how do they present themselves in the contemporary city, and what role do they play? What are their main features? Where in the city are they located? Are they all external, peripheral, situated at the edge of town, since they replace the traditional squares which no longer exist in the suburbs?

Perspectival section of the Baths of Diocletian, E. Paulin, 1880.

Or do they sprout up equally well in the city center, where abandoned buildings have now been renewed and redefined? Why is their role not an alternative to the square of yesterday but effectively interprets the possible squares of tomorrow?

At the same time the social expression of the new collective places changes too: they no longer have one meaning alone; above all, they must interpret the needs and methods of a changing society and be an expression of the many cultures that comprise our society. Change, flexibility and adaptability are the keywords of these spaces, expressing the present or, better, all the emotional features related to a finite, corporeal perception of time. Spectacle as a simulation or interpretation of reality; play as an expression of free time, which must be able to reach people in their most emotional, intimate, secret recesses, is an important feature of these new spaces, which can no longer be a conception of the world as an ethical expression of universal values, but as one of many conceptions of life. They can foreshadow possible impressions, grandeurs, dreams and also consolations, thus helping individuals to discover the various possible paths of their existence[4].

Photomontage of the Temple Mount in Jerusalem with a brise-soleil system. Y. Friedman, 1996.

They become places where individuals can experiment with different experiences, almost a concentrate of inner emotions and collective practices for reflecting on our lives, and they attempt to reappropriate the essential function which the great squares of antiquity had and which today no longer corresponds to the use that is commonly made of the spaces we continue to call squares.

The novelty of the phenomenon is also revealed in the difficulty of naming the new spaces that do not seem to have corresponding terms in the vocabulary of architecture. Names should reveal the interpretation and in some way the destiny of things, but here in reality we are faced with a conundrum: we do not have appropriate terms for describing the new collective urban places, or worse, we use them in a vague, neutral way to describe more complex phenomena[5].

We have seen how the problem immediately crops up when we use the very word square, which, having by now little or nothing in common with the concept as it refers to the traditional Italian piazze, must necessarily be redefined. The word square, in fact, in the modern world, has been used excessively and incorrectly, as an indication of any open space in the urban fabric, even if it is just a roundabout for cars or nothing more than an empty lot[6].

This terminological uncertainty is undoubtedly the sign of a more serious interpretive problem which leads us to consider the absolute necessity of broadening the notion of urban space to include new categories that go beyond the concept of single predetermined referents.

Even the adjective collective, which is used to define these places, no longer expresses, as is evident, multiple aggregates of people, categories or centers of interest, but at the same time effectively designates both the multiplicity of uses and that of the people who converge there.

Aerial view of Piazza Navona, Rome.

Aerial view of the CentrePompidou, R. Rogers and R. Piano, Paris, 1977.

Selfridges Center, Future System, Birmingham, 2003.

Introduction

NOTES

1 Jameson 1989.
2 Cenzatti, Crawford 1993.
3 "The birth of the city was due to a public need. Often it originated with a fence used for trade which subsequently was transformed into an open market, which still exists today among some small populations in Europe and South America.
It was the Greeks who invented the public place and made it the unique and essential condition of the city. Aristotle maintained that 'a city is made up of a number of citizens', those people with the right to participate in its legal and judicial functions. This was the polis, in which the city was the State and the State the city. The Romans expanded and modified this system: the State is a city (Rome), but this city does not comprise the whole State, which instead is made up of many cities. Politics and trade characterized the medieval city: in it public freedom was created in defiance of servitude to the nobility. The medieval town was the origin of the commune, hence of the res publica, namely of all and one and for one and all.
In the Renaissance city the public space was formalized further: in addition to streets, squares and fountains also acquired a definite value. The Baroque city, which cancelled out the communes, took over the public space as the property of the nation state.
Public spaces ceased being of one and all, and were now only for one and all.
The industrial city was not very different from the Baroque city as far as public spaces were concerned, although these decreased quantitatively and qualitatively. With time, capitals and other cities regained their communal character through the process of a power shift towards democracy. Nonetheless, in the secularized cities of the 20th century, indiscriminate allotments, bureaucratic difficulties, and the struggle between political, economic and social development led to the paradox of a greater democracy versus less public intervention through consultation and public decisions. The history of the city testifies to the concreteness and definiteness of the public place, which becomes a symbol and epitome of the city. Within the enormous space that it covers, the city expresses its nature in public places (both traditional and new). This expression helps to shape its identity and way of being. We believe however that the recovery of public places is the beginning of a phase that can lead us to reconstructing the public domain". Glusberg 1996, p. 280.
4 Sennett 1990.
5 Rocca 1996.
6 Panella 1997.

1 Evolution of new spaces

❝ *Moving from the acknowledgment of a gradual shift from a culture that operated according to processes determined by a logic of long-term development to a culture of instantaneity caused by the succession of events and global phenomena, Bonomi identifies three factors that yield new interpretative approaches to the present: the acceleration of events, the primacy of feelings, and the replacement of the concept of equality with that of freedom.* ❞

(F. Jameson)

Evolution of new spaces

"In the transition from modernity to post-modernity, the transformations experienced by the rules of games, the arts and therefore also architecture and the sciences since the end of the 19th century, but in very rapid and accelerated fashion since the end of the fifties, have profoundly altered the state of the culture and conditions of society as a whole" [1].

After a century in which we have mainly combated the scarcity of means for the certainty of ends, we find ourselves today in a completely reversed situation: contemporary society is characterized mainly by the affirmation of the 'end of ends', the death of the myth of means and, ultimately, by the absence of tension and struggle between two opposing world views.

The finalities or purposes that are at the source of experience are no longer given but demand constant decision; the powerful element of cohesion, such as ideology, which characterized the past, has been replaced by a way of life that for the most part is limited to seizing the opportunities offered by the present[2].

Starting with the affirmation that we are experiencing a gradual shift from a culture that operated according to processes determined by long-term developments, to a culture of instantaneity and simultaneity determined by a succession of global events and phenomena, Bonomi identifies three factors that offer new interpretations of this development: the acceleration of events, the primacy of feeling, and the substitution of the concept of equality with that of freedom.

This – especially in light of the acceleration of events – has been so sudden that it does not leave time to reflect on the past or make it possible to form predictions about the future, but only to work on the simultaneous nature of phenomena, which forces us to live in a continuous present. Working on the simultaneous nature of phenomena, in a sort of continuous present, also involves, according to Bonomi, renouncing the primacy of the rationality of the collective consciousness, in favor of a likewise collective primacy of feeling.

"Feeling is more important than understanding, because the simultaneous experiencing of a multiplicity leaves no time for reflection – that is to say, the mental work on the sequence of past-present- future – which is an integral part of understanding, leaves no time for personal feelings to mature and enter the marketplace of values and opinions, and requires that conduct follow up in live, real-time concurrency, 'a feeling put to work', used in response, whether adapting or not, to multiple events."

Centre Georges Pompidou, R. Rogers and R. Piano, Paris, 1977.

University library,
W. Arets, Utrecht, 2004.

Hence the phantasmagorical society, the society of the extraordinary, is characterized not by a radical absence of meaning but by its exact opposite: a proliferation of meanings. The subject, now free in his flux of experiences, is able to take possession of the images, symbols and rites of belonging that most convince and attract him, and reformulate them in autonomous fashion .

Thirdly, the present is marked by the change which has taken place in our world: from a mass society essentially struggling for the triumph of the principle of equality, we have passed on to a society that pursues the abolition of all those relative differences that do not allow everyone to develop his unique individuality. At the base of society there is no longer simply the development of equality, but the "development of the individual's freedom in terms of positive action, conduct against fear and against need". It can be said that the transition period is marked primarily by the shift from a vertical society, which promoted social relationships of a hierarchical type, linked however to a linear process, to a horizontal society, where social relationships insist on specific, particular environments, which move in parallel[3].

Collective places, in reflecting these changes, undergo this transformation in full. In a certain sense they attempt to elaborate the representative intentions of multiple identities, the identities of a population which, not recognizing itself in the subdivision into distinct social classes, and no longer having broad baggage of clearcut ideals to share, tends, as has already been observed, to identify itself in small groups, in restricted sets which are fragmented almost to the point of representing each single individual.

This social change we are describing has also produced a further change. In the past, collective places performed throughout the year the task of carrying out a series of activities that alternated in a somewhat broadened time-frame to include various stable, clearcut, unchanging functions which represented the characteristic features of society. These functions took place at fixed, well-marked intervals that were distributed in an orderly fashion during the year. The various activities were of both a secular and a religious kind, such as parades, various sorts of functions and religious occasions, recreational and leisure events related to the cycle of nature or to holidays, such as fairs, feast days, celebrations, balls, etc.

Today, the role of these places, along with our entire society, has changed. The frequency with which they represent and participate in social life is not as fixed and planned, and above all not as distinct. Today there are liable to be several needs that demand to be met simultaneously, and these places can be called upon to carry out tasks that are completely different, even within the time span of a single day. This is how apparently contrasting functions coexist and must be able to be absorbed and interpreted with the same degree of interest and intensity.

Our society constantly places before us the possibility of choice. Our path does not wend through fixed and preordained routes. Contemporary man is constantly an arbiter of the factors that can condition his existence. This holds true both for the work cycle and largely for how we spend our leisure time. This normally involves taking a more active attitude, a readiness for determining as far as possible one's own destiny and actions. What occurs in fact is just the opposite of what is often thought to be a feature of contemporary society, in which man appears to be passive, alone and in a continual state of subjection.

The places for relating have lost their main function of representing distinct values and sweeping everything into a single, overarching identity. Therefore they must be able to comprehend and interpret society's changing needs and undergo appropriate transformations. Consequently, they are places that, in expressing their capacity for constant change and evolution, and in having to be prepared for a multitude of uses and meanings, must live by their own vitality and be a magnet of emotional involvement, a powerhouse of suggestion that enables everyone to participate in the events that find in them a fertile opportunity for concentration. Their capacity to entertain, to arouse a sense of bewilderment and disorientation, becomes a fundamental feature as relational places, in addition to their capacity to simultaneously generate spectacle and game, to excite the imagination and make dreams seem true.

The meaning these places must convey also changes. There is no longer just one meaning; they must be able to satisfy not only multiple uses and functions variously combined, but also express and be ready to embrace different values. Hence today relational places must be able to predict and represent a wide range of possibilities, and indeed push the individual actively toward the broadest range of meanings he is seeking.

Nevertheless, there is undoubtedly some subtle thing that remains of one's own culture of place, in which they are inserted, and, contrary to what some claim, it seems reasonable to assume that these centers cannot have the same characteristics the world over and cannot be considered as non-places [4].

The centers must not be indifferent to the context in which they are inserted, in the sense that the uses, customs, traditions and memories of a particular place must contribute somehow to their definition. It is absolutely unthinkable that they should be complexes indifferent to their locale, and, as micro-cities unto themselves, replicable everywhere at random in the same way. On the contrary, they cannot avoid containing to some extent a particularity of place, a reinterpretation of customs, a revisitation of usages, perhaps utterly transformed in manner and form, but present in their incisiveness and expressive power.

Preferences in the modes of recreation and entertainment, of assembling and living in urban spaces, of organizing unusual events and understanding the collective memory, change too from one area to another. These factors must resurface to one extent or another in the formulation of public places, and must determine that subtle contour or subliminal suggestion which obviates the sense of unease when one crosses through and experiences, albeit in a thousand different ways, those new spaces for relating which have managed to preserve the soul of that place and understand that certain something which is unique to every city and small town, and which succeeds in making itself felt.

Chapter 1

Santa Caterina Market, EMBT Miralles-Tagliabue, Barcelona, 2005.

MyZeil Shopping Mall, Studio Fuksas, Frankfurt, 2009.

A day-long journey

Our era is characterized, among other things, by a total change in the concept and employment of leisure time. Leisure time, as a time not to devote to activities related to safeguarding the survival of the individual, can be identified in various ways: cultural activities, entertainment, sports, hobbies and travel, or all these things together. The concept was born and has developed since labor became a mere attribute of society and not its principal feature, and hence it can become a counterpart.

We have in fact come to spend our leisure time out of the home, condensing it into a few hours or into the space of a day. We tend to sample various types of experience, seeking the sensations of varied emotions, desiring to pack all possible situations together, living through something like a trip in a single day. Collective places can meet these new demands and therefore become the vehicle of a micro-trip.

A trip that is not necessarily to faraway places, but which can be a trip into the future or into the past, a trip into the world of telematics, into the world of science, a trip into the world of consumption and amusement – into an unknown, as yet undiscovered land. At the basis of this need there is a specific desire to identify with unusual situations, to choose the kind of country to visit, to experience what one desires to possess, in what way and for how long.

The increasing need of ordinary people to escape from their ordinary situations, and the increasingly frantic search for pleasurable experiences that are above all different from our everyday ones, leads to an ongoing desire to set out for someplace, or a take a short break from one's normal activities, to be engaged in novel stimulations, different from the daily grind, non-trivial and non-routine, in short to experience a spree of exceptions.

The crucial factor for the success of these places lies in the sampling of pleasures that involve different senses and that in any case do not refer to the scale of values typical of normal life. The individual must be able to find himself in a threshold state, almost outside of time and space, in an antistructure where his habitual ties are suspended and his daily obligations are absent. This gap between ordinary and extraordinary experience can occur in different ways .

On the one hand, normal activities can be carried out in an unusual visual environment. A different visual field and a new atmosphere can make normally trivial activities into something unique and attractive: sports, shopping, eating, drinking, taking a walk – all of this can take on a more vibrant and engaging aspect if the setting is not the one frequented on a daily basis:

"(...) Even when individuals seem to seek satisfaction in products, in their choice, purchase and use, the satisfaction comes from expectation, the pursuit of pleasure at the level of fantasy. The principal motivation of consumption in these places is therefore not just materialistic, as has always been thought; the aim of the individual is to experience 'in reality' the pleasurable situations of tension they have already experienced in their fantasy"[5].

On the other hand, in order for the visitor to enjoy these unusual activities, the available settings must offer him a wide variety of choice.

"Now he wants to contemplate something sacred; now something informative to expand his knowledge; now something beautiful, which ennobles it and makes it more refined; now something to relieve his boredom"[6].

By compressing distances one can sample a variety of situations that would otherwise be impossible. It is tantamount to traveling through time and space, simulating the effect of a time machine, where the spectator, in a willing suspension of disbelief, can feel the turmoil and excitement of experiencing it everything almost simultaneously, as well as choosing not to make a final choice that excludes other possible options. He can decide whether to have an experience in a typical country town, in an American skyscraper, or in a typical outdoor pub, and so on. Furthermore, he can decide to have more than one of them in rapid succession. Daydreaming and fantasizing new experiences become two processes that recur frequently in the contemporary way in which we experience consuming places.

At bottom the spectator must be allowed to move smoothly, without being tied to the constraints of a lofty culture and knowing he can roam at will in

Section of ships Orazio and Virgilio. (based on *I Transatlantici*, Genoa 2001)

search of the pleasure principle. The world is like a stage, and the fun lies in being able to choose to participate in an infinite number of possibilities.

This accidental tourist, as we shall call him, is however self-conscious, cool and aloof from roles, seeking more and more variegated forms and places of pleasure, rather than consolidating experiences and collective memories. He is on the prowl for a more varied and immediate pleasure, new and definitely out of the ordinary. There is an increasing tendency to assign a particular theme to these places, a theme that is not always necessarily linked to historical and geographical factors but may also be the result of imagination, or are inspired by historical and geographical conditions. In such thematic places or areas everything must seem absolutely real and authentic, and its true-to-lifeness is enhanced by the use of smells and sounds, and visual and atmospheric simulations. Thus these ambiences become more real than the originals, hyperreal, and experience becomes, as Eco says, a voyage in hyperreality.

"Thus representations are in keeping with our notions of reality and symbols, which we carry within us, waiting for them to be realized: (...) Disneyland, for example, tells us that fictitious nature corresponds much more to the demands of our daydreams. Disneyland tells us that technology can give us more reality of how nature can give us" [7].

The growing ability to create and invent new themes that seem more real than the originals makes it so that what is theorized in these centers becomes almost a "symbolic rejection of the world's geographical community", establishing a new collective sense of place based on "transcending the geographical barrier of space and distance. The world's real spatial relationships are thus replaced by other imaginary ones" [8].

As in performing normal activities in unusual environments, so in performing unusual activities, one is aware of the fact that this operation is a game, or a plurality of games, that have a multitude of texts, and that their entirety is unauthentic[9]. The visitor knows he is living unreal experiences and often derives a greater satisfaction from feeling just "like a child", where the game imposes an implicit acceptance of useless rules[10] and where there is a special pleasure in violating "small taboos in various forms of consumption, such as eating or drinking to excess, spending money recklessly or dressing extravagantly, maintaining a variety of temporal rhythms, and so on."

Instant City, Archigram, 1969.

Chapter 1

28

Play as an experience outside of daily life

The game experience is one of the levels of interpretation of public spaces because it corresponds to the nature of distraction, entertainment, but also of liberation that the complex type of spatial knowledge must provide.

It is an experience that, as we have seen, presents itself as a parallel, independent activity, as opposed to the actions and decisions of normal[11] life, through characteristics that are unique to it. Game takes a different approach to reality since it remains a space unto itself, separate from ordinary life, a closed, protected universe[12]. In a pure circumscribed space and at a time established a priori by precise, arbitrary but seeingly irrevocable rules that must be accepted as such, a free, completely desired experience unfolds which has the characteristics of an oasis.

"The term 'game' thus combines in a kind of experience the idea of limit, freedom and invention. Game is viewed as an attempt to replace the normal confusion of real situations with the idea of an island, the transition from a chaotic and uncontrollable universe to an orderly universe that rests on a coherent and balanced system defined by 'rights and duties, privileges and responsibilities.'"[13]

Through this kind of experience, we have in these places the sensation of standing on a kind of neutral ground where, as in the Disney experience, we enter a world in which we play on an equal footing, where from the start we all become equal and where a near situation of catharsis seems to be established: all the players start out from scratch, in the same condition, and can all take the trip in conditions of equality, each determining his own destiny through a series of choices unrestricted by basic conditions.

The game experience is an integral part of these places-events, but it goes beyond the appearance of a merely happy world apart, a carefree oasis of joy where one can take refuge, and is instead, as Caillois defines it, the territory of "an uncertain island".

The very expression expose yourself, take up the challenge, presumes that we are prepared for an illusory dimension which in itself is already unstable and which urges us to participate in risk and in a state of excitement. Game is, according to Roger Caillois, an intense, disturbing experience characterized by continuously startling elements whose four main features are: chance, competition, mask and vertigo. Game is something like a "turning platform with different sides and aspects from which part extreme diagonals, the diagonal of overwhelming strength and intelligence, the dispossessing one

of the function of mask, and the one of the abysses that fate and vertigo allow us to skirt."

The profound bewilderment is deliberately accepted;

"Feeling pleasure in the face of panic, exposing yourself spontaneously to trying not to surrender to it, having before your eyes an image of destruction, knowing it is inevitable and having no way out except pretended indifference is, as Plato says in reference to another gamble, a fascinating risk worth taking[14]."

Olivandenhof, HPP Hentrich-Petschnigg & Partner, Cologne, 1988.

Chapter 1

The game metaphor as an ambiguous element is at the same time self-justification and self-struggle, calculation and capacity to overcome obstacles, but also sidestep, surprise, novelty, and so too excess and exhilaration. This ambivalent scenario determined by the flow from one effect to another, and by complementary and polar effects, certainly offers one level of insight into these places.

At bottom, this metaphor contains embryonically a whole series of connotations and a number of hints that shed light on and stress its possibilities. The most direct seem to be disguise and vertigo, which introduce a more liberating aspect of imbalance and bewilderment, those aspects most closely related to the less cerebral, more sensory and emotional aspect[15].

Pleasure, as in the more codified and perhaps also more stereotyped Disney experiences, is afforded by the feeling of elation one feels in placing his identity in danger through a sidestep, a bewilderment, an issuing out of oneself, out of one's usual roles, to become something and someone else, and thus feeling the effect that mask and pretence have on us and on others. Even the overall experience one has in the sensation of vertigo, understood as complete abandon, as loss of the sense of limits, is one of the aspects of these places; nothing more, in the end, than the desire to destroy the stability of perception and to subject one's consciousness to a lucid, sensual panic, a kind of trance, a kind of bewilderment.

The game experience revolves mainly around the pleasure of winning something, of placing oneself somehow in danger, of overcoming an obstacle that is in any case fictitious, approachable, and so at bottom almost harmless.

"Game, along with all these unreal places, selects its field of action and its difficulties, isolates them from the context and so makes them unreal[16]."

The game experience, which at bottom is an activity defined as free, since clearly the choice of playing is a free choice, is separate because circumscribed within strict temporal and spatial limits; uncertain because we don't know in advance how it will end; unproductive, regulated because it is subject to new conventions and an established, fictitious order, as it is completely unreal. It is configured in all these manifestations as an authentic simulation of real life.

Man has always found great pleasure in disguising himself, in wearing a mask, in playing a role while losing his sense of orientation, and changing identity; in this game of dissembling reality and simulating another reality there is a continuous invention and discovery of new territories.

Sony Center, J. Murphy, Berlin, 2000.

Chapter 1

32

Theater as a simulation of reality

The statement that today's society is image-based has become a near cliché. Yet it is a true and particularly effective statement. Already Guy Debord argued that images have become increasingly predominant not only as an increasingly prevalent presence and influence in advertising and TV, but also and above all as a mediating tool of social relationships, so that everything that is directly lived has been transferred into a representation[17]. Such a total predominance of spectacle determines a loss of immediate experience. Living in an era of simulation leads us increasingly to replace experience with a surrogate: its representation[18].

In reality, the splitting in two carried out by representation, which can appear as a surrogate of direct experience, as a mere passive condition of automatic spectator reception, can be translated into new potentials for designing public places. Spectacle too can become an active instance of communication. The user can be called upon to take a stand. He can choose a direction, confront experiences (more or less virtual), and get actively involved. Spectacle becomes a form of active spatial experience that enriches normal experiences but does not replace them.

These places, having become themselves great theaters of consumption, of exchange of goods and information, of the images and culture of contemporary society, must be able to spur the visitor on to involve himself in their complexity, experiencing it actively and energetically, and not merely enduring it in total passivity.

The experience of living in such intense, variegated places, which are the hallmark of today's society, offering the ambiguity and uncertainty of game, the continuous and ever-changing interaction between reality and fiction, truth and duality typical of spectacle, must be able to generate a formative, liberating experience, interpreting our society's multiple perspectives and offering a broad spectrum of possibilities, where people can enjoy the emotions and sensations they want when they want them. These can be places of consolation over against the more sterile and harsh reality of the outside world, which the individual is more often than not forced to endure and where his leeway is almost always very tight.

"The history of public buildings is marked, beyond their functional, economic and technical aspects, by the urge to create spaces of illusion which enhance cultural and civic life to the point of its becoming a collective event. Only with this touch of fantasy can a public building provide space for the hopes that yank the citizen out of his armchair and his daily routine. It is precisely this that, according to Richard Sennett marks the sphere of public life and allows people to change their roles."[19]

Thus today public places have - though actually, to varying degrees, they have always had - the role of creating spaces for illusion, imagination and stimulation of creativity. Spaces that are a stage on which emotional and perceptual adventures can be acted out, and where, as in a global theater, visitors are at once actors and spectators, and where these roles are continually interchangeable[20]. This enables these places to become a platform for collective events that all can take part in, that provide stimulation and enrichment and an opportunity for both individual and collective expression, in a constant play between reality and make-believe.

Apropos of this, it should be noted that Baudrillard calls attention to a particular aspect of this predominance of the image in his analysis of the feverish, pervasive communication which marks our age and society, pointing out that all events, spaces and memories are absorbed into the single dimension of information, and that "we are continually subjected to a forced extroversion of all interiority and a forced introjection of all exteriority, which the categorical imperative of communication signifies."

He argues that there no longer exists the charm of what is hidden, removed, obscure, but since everything is "all visible, too visible, more visible than invisible", it turns into what he provocatively labels as obscenity, an absence of mystery, something that no longer harbors any secrets and hidden sides, and so is entirely soluble in information and communication. Ob-scenity, in the root sense of the term, signifying a horrible or unpleasant action that was not represented in ancient Greek theater, but only narrated, and so took place offstage, begins precisely when there is no illusion, when everything becomes transparent and instantly visible, subjected to the harsh, inexorable light of information and communication.

Therefore, what most characterizes today's world is not so much a loss of reality, as this absolute proximity and total instantaneity of things, a kind of overexposure to the transparency of the world[21].

Everything is abandoned to transparency, which is why there is no transcendence and no possibility of suppression or transgression. Hyper communication translates into a huge saturation of meaning which is consumed by its own success, without play, secrecy or distance. In this way information no longer refers to an event but becomes a promotion of information itself as warning, and so there is the risk of shifting from a society of spectacle to one of mere ceremony.

Excess of communication, the constant flow of information, transparency as a ubiquitous phenomenon, regulate our lives heavily at every moment. There is a whole series of excessively aggressive and visible elements. Everything is within easy reach, the media are increasingly present, advertising increasingly overbearing. We are conditioned by an omnipresent cyber-culture raised to the nth power, as well as by a science that to create progress ends up depriving us of our natural defenses.

In this situation, architecture can play a crucial role by providing the means, places and spaces in which to retrieve, our hidden side, the part of us that is linked to imagination[22]

The design of these collective spaces cannot shirk this goal, cannot avoid demanding and enabling the chance to have experiences that stimulate feeling and fantasy[23] and suggest the power of seeing what is actually not there, recovering our hidden realm, the realm of illusion linked to imagination, discovery and, why not, to magic[24].

NOTES

1 Lyotard 1979.
2 The present becomes the only way to read the past and the future. We are as yet unable to grasp the fact that the past no longer aids us in "forging and changing characters, settling cohesion and recognition within common reference points, and above all to form the historical present of a people." Bonomi 1996.
3 "The passing of this era, which insists on the fabric of representation, is marked by the transition from a vertical to a horizontal society.
- The vertical society was one that, founded on the centrality of the forms of productive, assembly-line labor, delineated social relationships of a hierarchical type, with centralized, relatively homogeneous representations from the center to the periphery of the system. It was characterized by the paradigm of equality and by a symbiotic society-state relationship.
- The horizontal society is one in which social relations insist on particular areas of territory, gender and non-hierarchical interests, in a linear process from the periphery to the center, of polyarchy, and produce representations that exhaust their action within those 'special' areas, at times without assuming the general interests of rationality as its aim. It is characterized by the paradigm of freedom and by territorial positioning seen as a strategic resource midway between local and global." Bonomi 1996, p. 55.
4 Augé 1992.
5 Seneca comments that already in imperial Rome travel was the exclusive activity of a small circle of people. Two centuries of uninterrupted peace favored the development of an authentical travel network, by which it became possible to travel from Hadrian's Wall to the Euphrates, "(...) and this enabled city dwellers to experience constantly new sensations and pleasures (...) one seeks what arouses intense pleasure, what strikes the different senses from those normally used, and nourishes daydreams and imagination." Urry 1995, p. 19.
6 Feiler 1985, p. 269.
7 Eco 1986, p. 44.
8 Imagine visiting Disneyland, Malibu Beach, Bourbon Street, the San Diego Zoo, Rodeo Drive in Beverly Hills, and the Great Barrier Reef in Australia on one weekend and under one roof. Touted as the largest complex of its kind in the world, the center covers 110 acres and includes 828 stores, 110 restaurants, 19 theaters, a 5-acre

water park with a glass dome that towers over 19 floors. Admire the lake inside the center, complete with 4 submarines from which you can see sharks, octopuses, tropical marine life and a reconstruction of the Great Barrier Reef. The Fantasyland Hotel rooms boast a variety of themes: on one floor are the ancient Roman rooms, on another Arabic rooms from 'The Arabian Nights', Polynesian rooms." Urry, 1995, p. 206.

9 For example, in England there is a center in Gateshead Metrocentre which is Urry describes like this in his book: "(...) it contains three miles of mall with 300 shops, 40 restaurants, a 10-screen cinema, a bowling alley, a huge fantasy realm full of games and entertainment venues, a kindergarten and three thematic areas. The themes are: 'The old Village', a water mill with fake plastic ducks on the pond, a 'Roman Forum ' with areas in which you can recline in the Roman manner, and a 'Mediterranean Village' with Italian, Greek and Lebanese restaurants alongside a winding scenic Mediterranean road. In this place, of course, shopping is only part of the lure of the mall, which features mainly leisure and tourism. On a short walk you can enjoy a wide range of tourist attractions, go for a stroll, looking and making yourself look as if 'on vacation', and try out many entertainment facilities." Urry 1995, p. 207.

10 Feiler 1985.

11 In 1939 Johan Huizinga wrote the first contemporary classic on the game theme, claiming that games are a crucial factor of every culture and that, if we dig a little, we find that the world of games and the sacred world belong to the same universe: "(...) the game is action, or voluntary occupation, carried out within certain confined limits of time and space, according to voluntarily accepted rules, and yet engages in an absolute manner, which has an end in itself, accompanied by a sense of tension and joy, and the consciousness of 'being different ' from ' ordinary life' ". Huizinga, 1939, p. 55.

12 "Games interrupt the rhythm of daily habits. They project the player into an imaginary space and time that redefine the reality of his world, establishing a special condition of his emotions and feelings. Among adults the most habitual games, not surprisingly, are those that place money at risk, while for young people games have always assumed an infinite variety of forms, in which everyday rules are transgressed". Zecchi, 1996, p. 63.

13 "Games, in theory, seem to have no meaning outside of themselves, and therefore their rules are pre-established and absolute; beyond all discussion we play only play if we want, when we want, for as long as we like; the 'game' as such is a free activity". Caillois 1967, p. 23.

14" Is all this sufficient for arguing that the transition to civilization strictly defined involves the gradual elimination of this joint primacy of risk and mimicry, and its substitution with the pre-eminence in social relations with the pair agonalea, competition and chance? However, whether as cause or consequence, whenever a great culture manages to emerge from its original chaos, there is a significant regression of the forces of simulacrum and giddiness. They are then emptied of their historical significance, pushed to the edge of public life, reduced to increasingly modest and intermittent, if not downright illegal and unlawful, roles, or else confined within limited and regulated games and fantasy, where they grant the same eternal gratifications, but consistently repressed, and now prone to distract people from their boredom or relax them from their fatigue, with neither madness nor delirium". Caillois 1967, p. 117.

15 "The tangled and confused laws of ordinary life are replaced, within this circumscribed space and established time, with precise, arbitrary, irrevocable rules that we must accept as such and which govern the proper conduct of the game. The game has no meaning other than itself. It is precisely for this reason that its rules are mandatory and absolute, beyond discussion. There is no reason for them to be as they are, rather than in some other way. Those who do not accept them with this peculiarity must necessarily judge them as pure whimsy . Caillois 1967, p. 23.

16 "The fairs and amusement parks where disguises are not usually worn are in compensation those devoted pre-eminently to the occasions, pitfalls and attractions of vertigo.

These fenced off areas contain the essential features of play fields. They are separated from the surrounding space through arcades, swags, garlands, ramps and neon signs, poles, flags, decorations of all kinds, visible from afar, and which mark the boundaries of a sacred universe. Beyond that barrier, you find yourself in a world curiously richer and more full of life than the everyday world: a noisy and excited crowd, a riot of light and color, a continuous, exhausting pandemonium which is bewildering and where everyone loves to shout at his neighbor or seeks to draw attention to himself; a bustle that encourages carefreeness, confidence, chat, good-natured boldness. All this lends a unique liveliness to the general atmosphere. In addition, in the case of fairs, their cyclical nature adds to the spatial break a temporal scansion which counters the monotony of daily existence with a moment of frenzy. Fairs and amusement parks appear to be the proper sphere of the instruments of vertigo, mechanisms of rotation, oscillation, suspension, fall, specially designed to provoke a visceral panic. But all the game categories are present in amusement parks, with their multiple seductions." Caillois, 1967, pp. 155-156.

17 "Spectacle is not a collection of images but a social relationship among individuals, mediated by images ... The entire life of societies in which modern conditions of production prevail presents itself as an immense accumulation of spectacles. Everything that was

Chapter 1

directly experienced has been distanced into a representation". Debord, 1971, p. 85-86.

18 "Within this set of problems is the theme of the architectural object and its role in urban life: public or collective buildings are an event, a particular point of reference in the context of complex urban structures. Where the functional and architectural structures of neighborhoods display the normality of urban life, these objects are the exception. (...) The function of a building at the time and place of its birth is the prerequisite for the formulation of its them, a necessary condition for the purpose of understanding it, as well as, in my view, an element of the discipline of formal discussion. Boullée was convinced that 'our buildings, especially the public ones, should be in a certain sense poems. The external impression they make on our senses should be able to awaken in us the same feelings that awaken the purpose for which they were built'". Brenner 1990, pp. 13-15

19 Sennett 1977.

20 "Going back in time, we must consider public/collective places in their historical origins as a stage for the celebration of collective myths, tracing the collective (public) elements of cities and the institution of theaters from the same beginnings; this includes not only the concept of 'scenic drama', but also the transcendence of the categorical division between stable, real urban space and temporary, illusory theatrical space". Brenner, 1990, p. 21.

21 Baudrillard continues to ask himself: what is left of the "seduction, passion of this power that tears human beings away from any location or objective definition? What remains of this fatality or supreme irony, this aspiration to evasion or alternative strategy?" Baudrillard 1987, p. 32. "Stripped of any setting and penetrated without any obstacle, they cannot produce the limits of their own beings, cannot produce themselves as a mirror. They become a purs screen, a pure surface of absorption and reabsorption of networks of influence." Ibid., p. 16

22 Of interest in this regard is what Richard Sennett writes: "(...) good intentions do not reveal to the urban planner a truth that is well-known to writers: you cannot undertake anything significant by creating something that immediately embodies its full and complete sense. Let us return to our original problem, invention and discovery. How can urban planning invent ambiguity and the ability to create surprises? It must translate into visual terms the elements that contribute to creating a narrative beginning. The beginning of a novel cancels and conceals something; to create a space it is necessary to act in the same way, by cancelling and concealing, through actions that favor continuous movement. (...) The 'personal character' of an urban space, like a character in a novel, is developed through a series of continual changes and clashes. This experience of displacement and resistance exists in the arts, but is absent from the urban planning" . Sennett 1990, p. 211-219.

23 "And here the problem is to understand: what will the future of the individual imagination be in what we are accustomed to calling the 'civilization of the image'? In an age in which we are bombarded with images of all kinds, paradoxically, we must not lose the capacity to fantasize, the power to focus on visions with our eyes closed, to imagine worlds, to think in terms of images so that these become well-defined, self-sufficient forms. Once an individual's visual memory was limited to the heritage of his direct experiences and a modest repertory of images reflected from his culture; the ability to shape personal myths arose from the way in which the fragments of this memory were combined with each other in unexpected, suggestive juxtapositions. Today we are bombarded with such a vast amount of images that we are no longer able to distinguish direct experience from what we have seen for a few seconds on television. Our memories are buried under layers of shattered images, like a garbage dump, where it is increasingly difficult for any one figure to emerge from the mass. We are no longer able to perform the mental act of assembling stories, to interpret scenes in various ways, produce variants, contaminate stories, merge episodes into a larger story. Let us say that different elements combine to form the visual part of the literary imagination: the direct observation of the real world, the transfiguration of dream and fantasy, the figurative world transmitted by culture at its various levels, and a process of abstraction, condensation and internalization of sensory experience, of decisive importance as much in visualizing as in verbalizing thought." Calvino 1993, p. 106.

24 "This aspect of spectacle, which should directly concern the design process, could become with its constructive mechanisms and its great, if perhaps somewhat reductive power, a new starting point for finding possible roles for architecture". Bordini 1994, p. 32.

2 Evolutions in the ways of living the aesthetic experience

" Humanity, precisely because it has a body with its particular needs and requirements, has an urgency to touch things and feel them. Virtual space deprives us of these ties, because it is a mental space. So it will be the continuous consumption of the experience of a virtual space that, by contrast, will lead us to a fuller and more conscious reappropriation of the sensory relationship with the real city. "

(A. Bonomi)

Bodys Isek Kingelez, Kimbembele Ihunga, Kimbéville 1993-94 paper, mixed materials, H. 130 cm; L. 240 cm; 1993-94.

Evolutions in the ways of living the aesthetic experience

The decline of a unitary idea of history and the consequent crisis of the idea of progress have shown that, since no unified course of human events exists, we cannot even argue that they proceed toward a single end and realize and enact a rational, predetermined plan. The European ideal of

Binoculars building, F. O. Gehry e C. Oldenburg, Venice California, 1999.

humanity becomes one among many and cannot have universal relevance. The concept of a unitary, centralized history does not exist, but instead shifts according to one's point of view. The advent of the communication society has undoubtedly contributed to expanding our awareness of the many different visions of the world. The intensified possibilities of relaying information about events in nearly real time increasingly contradicts the idea that there is only one reality.

The idea that at any given moment we can be absolutely sure of how things stand is being replaced by the ideal of emancipation, based on the categories of oscillation, plurality and the concept of erosion of the very principle of reality[1].

But how can this be considered a positive development? Or rather, what is the positive, emancipating compensation for the loss of the reality principle? Its innovative, explosive force lies in the possible coexistence of the wide gamut of cultural, ethnic, religious and aesthetic diversity which it creates. Each one speaks out and takes shape, generating an effect of bewilderment caused by the awareness that each of these systems is relative and that this is much more important than the mere identifying effect of these differences.

The emancipated effect of the confusion of dialects can be found in the description of the aesthetic experience Wilhelm Dilthey suggests: how an encounter with a work of art is a way to gain experience, explore the imagination and new forms of existence, experience other ways of life different from the usual ones[2]. The aesthetic experience has the capacity to give life to other worlds beyond our horizon and to bring forth a reflection on the relativity and contingency of our real world.

Living in this plurality of cultures, in this manifold world "means experiencing freedom as a continuous oscillation between belonging and disorientation". Already philosophers such as Heidegger and Nietzsche had shown how being does not coincide with what is stable and fixed, but rather, if anything, identifies itself with events, dialogue, interpretation, and how this translates into an experience of oscillation rather than a firm, stationary one. The relationship between art and everyday life has undergone a thorough transformation, which can be appreciated if one thinks of the shift from an ideal of utopia to a form of heterotopia, to borrow Foucault's happy phrase[3].

The term utopia was understood as the tendency to identify aesthetic significance with existential meaning, as in the early twentieth century avant-garde experience, where every work called into question the very essence of art[4].

Utopia, even in the context of aesthetics, presupposed the conviction that there was a unified course of history and that the aesthetic experience of the recognition of beauty was in itself a way of reconfirming one's identification with the values of that particular community. With the advent of the mass society there has been no general adoption of the aesthetic values of the cultural elite, but rather a multiplicity of ideas about what constitutes beauty, opening the way to the expression of other cultures and other worlds. The concept of a unitary world, which was the keystone of science, has been replaced by a multiplicity of different worlds. The ability of an artwork to be earthshaking is now increasingly thought of in a pluralistic, heterotopic sense.

Dilthey already indicated a profound new sense of the aesthetic experience in his capacity to make us live in an imaginary dimension, in other possible existences, thus expanding the boundaries of our daily existence.

The transition from a utopian concept to a heterotopic one restores the aesthetic dignity of ornament and lightness of being. Or rather, we discover that ornament is almost the very essence of the aesthetic experience, the very meaning of the heterotopia of the aesthetic experience.

The aesthetic entity of the mass society contains a plurality of ornaments. The fact that its aesthetic products are ephemeral and subject to an unceasing eclecticism, that it is difficult to find in them anything essential, and that the element of kitsch is ever-present, actually corresponds to the essence and style of art in the present age[5].

For this reason aesthetic experiences that are heterotopian and abound in ornament are no longer traceable to a metaphysical knowledge of being that is stated in its features of stability, presence and structure, but present themselves as difference, as always being in addition something else, with their characteristic effect of continual disorientation and alienation.

The sharp reversal by which culture occupies a more central position in the organization of society has produced a progressive breakdown of the difference between 'high culture' and 'low culture', and between the diversity of cultural forms, such as tourism, art, education, music, shopping, cinema, theater, television, sports, photography, and architecture itself.

In a complex of relations between signifier, significance and referent, late-modern society is characterized primarily by a system of meanings whose fundamental structural feature is dedifferentiation[6].

Modernism has always implied above all a structural differentiation, and hence the development of various institutional and normative areas such as the economy, the family, the state, science, morality and aesthetics, and each of these has always been subject to what Weber called self-legislation.

Render of some characteristic item of Eurdisney: *Sleeping Beauty castle*, *space shuttle* and the *Feature Animation Building* by R. Sternn.

This differentiation concerned the various cultural spheres at both the horizontal and vertical levels while contemporary society is characterized by the tendency to dedifferentiate, understood as a fusing of the aesthetic aspect with the experience of everyday life; a fusion that has some special features.

On the one hand, the breach of the barriers between cultural and public objects, which allows for a continuous interactivity, an active participation of spectators, its beneficiaries, whether it is a museum, a show or any form of entertainment, in which they are continually called upon to take part[7].

On the other hand, there is the breakdown of the boundaries between artistic and commercial production, which intertwines culture and commerce in an almost constant, indissoluble fashion.

Finally, there is a very tight relationship between reality and representation. Meaning is determined more and more by figurativeness or visuality, and by an increasing proportion of referents of meaning, which make up reality, are themselves representations. As Baudrillard notes, "we consume more and more signs or representations. Social identities are constructed through the exchange of signs-values, in a 'show-biz' spirit. For example, people know that the media are a simulation and in turn they simulate the media".

In this world of signs and spectacle there is no true originality but only, in the words of Umberto Eco, trips into hyperreality. Everything is a copy, a text based on another text, and what is false seems more real than reality[8].

Bewilderment and swing

The aesthetic experience is particularly significant for an understanding of "the sense of being", or rather the salient features of existence; it is essential to reflect on the new way a work of art proffers itself, which today goes beyond the traditional metaphysical definition of art as a place of reconciliation, the correspondence between inner and outer, of catharsis.

Already Benjamin in The Work of Art in the Age of Mechanical Reproduction, argued that the new conditions of production and artistic enjoyment that have developed in our mass media society have significantly changed its essence, its way of proffering itself in the present age. In speaking of cinema, which he considered the most characteristic art form of the era of technical reproducibility, he identified an effect on the viewer which he defined as shock[9].

Heidegger too, in his essay The Origin of the Work of Art, identified in the word stoss, literally "impact", the effect of the work of art on the observer.

The thesis advanced by Vattimo is that, in following the development that includes and links up the two terms stoss (Heidegger), and shock (Benjamin), we can grasp the essential features of the new essence of art in late-industrial society. The two concepts certainly have one element in common in their fundamental character of disorientation. The aesthetic experience, therefore, becomes an experience centered primarily on the concept of alienation, which requires continuous readjustment. Its objective is not a condition of final recomposition, but is aimed at keeping the disorientation alive, not just temporarily but as a constitutive state.

In late modernity, oscillation is an inherent feature of the aesthetic experience: the continuing effect of disorientation that one has toward any world, whether real or represented in a work of art[10].

"A work of art functions as a window of truth because it is an 'event' of being, which however has its event-essence in its being overwhelmed and 'dispossessed' in the play of mirrors of the world" [11].

Contemporary society has always seen, in the advent of the mass media and the growing possibility of ever more rapid communication, a consequent massification, a manipulation of consent. Instead, in the introduction of this new potentiality, we glimpse something that can be transformed into a positive factor, an alternative possibility produced by the fact that a greater mobility and hence a greater velocity of experience, goes against the tendency toward generalized domination and weakens the very notion of reality and of the entire conditioning and coercive force of the concept of absolute.

The society of spectacle, in addition to being, as the situationists see it, "the society of appearances manipulated by the powers that be"[12], is at the same time a society in which reality presents itself with softer, more fluid features, and in which experience can acquire the attributes of oscillation, disorientation, game, which make it particularly complex and liberating. Ambiguity becomes a feature of non-provisional aesthetic experience and is one more possibility by which the subject can attain to a fuller and more conscious appropriation of language.

Thus, in contrast to what was a nostalgia for the eternal life of a work of art and for the authenticity of experience, it must be understood that what remains of the creativity of art in the era of widespread communication is precisely disorientation, and that, to return to the two concepts of Benjamin and Heidegger, these are nothing more than a quest for a mobility and hypersensitivity of feeling and intelligence of metropolitan man.

An art that is no longer centered on the work itself but on the experience one may derive from it, even in terms of multiple but continuous variations, corresponds to this particular prevalence of excitability and hypersensitivity.

The mass media have instilled a sense of precariousness and superficiality that has hit hard against the prejudices of a traditionally idealizing aesthetic with reference to the work of art, considered a monumentum aere perennius. In this way the media end up favoring an aesthetic experience that involves the subject in a profound and authentic way, whether as creator or spectator, in all its manifestations, giving priority to sensitivity and emotion.

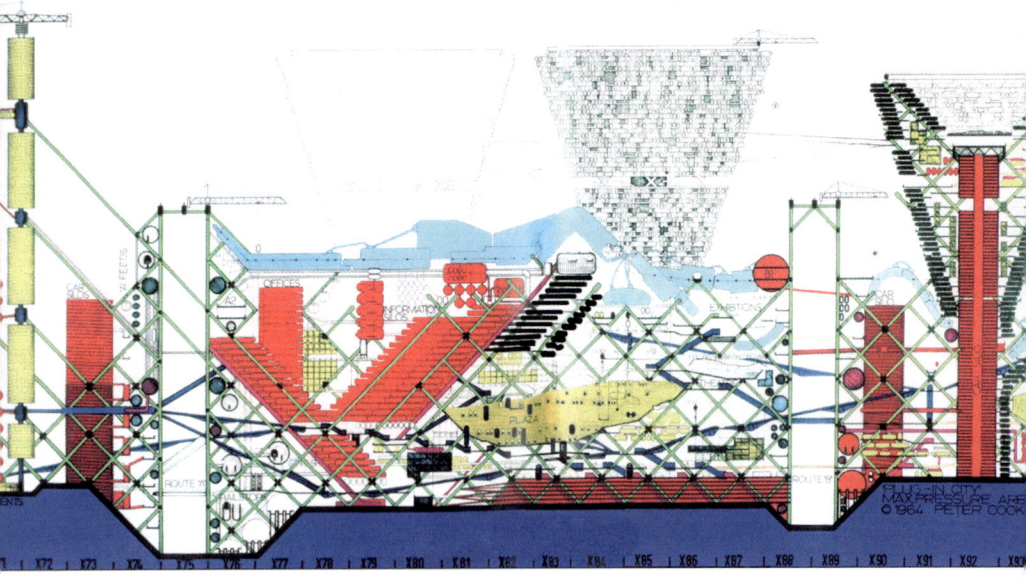

Plug-in City, P. Cook, 1964.

Chapter 2

A more sensitive and emotional approach

Every era has identified with concepts and keywords that have emphatically expressed its sensitivity and emotional tone. The seventeenth century explored passion, the eighteenth century sentiment, the nineteenth century the spirit and the heart, the first half of the twentieth century life. What are today's standards of feeling? "(...) The air gets tense, slippery, unstable, ambiguous: in music, the arts, the media, the antennas of collective feeling pick up hitherto unknown forms of experience and perceive the familiar ones as distorted beyond recognition. When every consumer item must be presented as exciting, daring, biting, it is a sign that the collective imagination of society is undergoing profound changes, which need urgently to be examined." All this implies a profound transformation of the very concept of art, whose starting point may lie in Hegel's definition of art forms as symbolic.

Perniola maintains that in this way two seemingly contradictory approaches of criticism intertwine: one directed towards the most advanced technological developments, such as the mechanical reproduction of works of art, videomatics and electronics, and the other directed towards the more emotional dimensions of experience, anthropology and possession.

Actually, we seek in our videomatic present a past of joy and variety of experience, and in our anthropological past a present of reproducibility and repetition. The technological and anthropological trends are diametrically opposed to what characterized them in the first half of the twentieth century. Technology has been stripped of its futuristic, Promethean will to world possession, and anthropology has been freed of its nostalgia for authentic origins[13].

In some forms of artistic and social expression elements have been borrowed from distant cultures, with appropriations from folk cultures, which have provided inspiration and strength from the mixture of different cultures and different languages. Thus works have been produced that belong to an intermediate culture, useful for a possible social consensus because they combine a high, intellectualized, cerebral culture with the more spontaneous, genuine expressions typical of popular culture, which regain an immediacy and participation discernible in certain emotional expressions of architecture, music and popular theater. Examples of this are Robert Wilson for theater, and Peter Gabriel, Brian Eno and Philip Glass for music, evidence of the way in which different artistic expressions are experiments of a fusion of multiple genres that produce a sense of disorientation, bewilderment and dream.

The various elements, originating from different cultures, are, of course, expertly contaminated. In music, the art that seems to interpret this phenomenon most successfully, one current has researched in recent years distant musical expressions that, while not native to us, are charged with a powerful liberating, instinctive, emotional force. Expressions of cultures different from and perhaps more primitive and gestural than our own, or traditional folk expressions (such as ballads, songs, refrains) undergo sophisticated intellectual re-elaborations in which they get combined with contemporary hi-tech effects or with names and words drawn from completely extraneous contexts.

The results obtained are striking and have opened the way for a new method of making music that interprets masterfully the needs, desires and expressions of our time.

The way we make contact with reality is changing. We are no longer inclined to adopt a structural approach to knowledge of the world and of culture, but opt rather for a sensory, emotional, impressionistic approach, a return to a more direct, instinctive relationship with reality, through taste, smell, touch and sound[14].

Humanity, precisely because it has a body with its own particular priorities, feels the need to touch things, to hear them. Virtual space deprives us of these links just because it is a purely mental space. Therefore it is this constant experience of a virtual space itself that, paradoxically, will lead us to a fuller and more conscious reappropriation of the sensory relationship with the real city[15].

"There is a growing consensus that Western culture must rediscover the possibility of all-involving emotional experiences of a positive and non-transgressive kind, which manifest themselves in non-pathological forms compatible with everyday functions"[16].

Public spaces, precisely as expressions of collective practices of relating in a given society at a given time, must contribute to reviving, exploiting and positively interpreting the potential of the emotional, participatory and active sphere in a certain social environment.

Having given new impetus to escapism and distraction and to all kinds of flight from reality, they must reflect on the variety of emotional and instinctual approaches to what is not directly rational, to the range of game, fantasy, imagination, dreams, the relationship with the senses, emotion and instinct. The difficulty lies in knowing how to interpret and then translate

into the architecture, design and construction of these spaces, something which in itself is not preordained, a non-rule, a non-a-priori definition that characterizes these aspects and whose results are as yet unknown.

It is not possible to determine all the facets of these issues because they are conditioned by a constant emotional interaction, an instinctive, sensory participation on the part of those who visit, use or frequent these places.

The design of the spaces we are delineating in their essence and finality, made even more complex by the fact that these emotional aspects, beyond depending on the constant interaction and participation between space-event-visitor, are hard to enumerate and define because of the constant additional components that in the past were perhaps neglected and forgotten, or probably supervened by other situations, places and events.

Discoveryland - New Orleans, Poster for Disneyland Paris, J. Michaelson, M. Johnston and R. Ziscis, 2000.

An experience "truer than the truth itself"

The study of the transformation of public places must not overlook the Disney phenomenon, which was born in the United States and later exported to Europe, near Paris; hence something that interests us directly. As we have seen with other forms of art which fuse various types of artistic and non-artistic expressions that lean more and more towards a levelling between high culture and the most naïve, traditional culture, this experience too can be collocated in the cultural mix of disoriention and alienation. Even if we cannot fail to note at once that here the union of architectural expression with cartoons is achieved through a full and complete transposition of that imaginary world, without the indispensable work of revision and adaptation that is fundamental to an authentic and fruitful fusion of different cultures.

Disney's original idea was to create a world of people in which the nostalgia for the past and the fervor of the present were seen through the eyes of the imagination: a place of warmth, nostalgia, and bright, sunny illusion. He had grasped the importance and the need for a clearcut visual message and felt that communication is clear and more explicit when it states what it displays[17]. All this is concentrated in a single enclosure where you pay to let yourself be lulled by these experiences. There is a sharp spatial separation from the rest, according to a principle of expositional enclosure. A contributing factor to this exceptional atmosphere is the elimination of automobiles in favor of efficient means of electric transportation with which one can move about freely[18].

The aim of Disneyland was vacation-fun-escapism, the program of "flight from everyday life to the lands of encounter"[19].

In the Disney world the pedestrian is king. Cars are abandoned before entering so that visitors can prepare themselves psychologically to enter a different world and at once accept the game they are playing, which quickly turns into a fairytale.

These places, consecrated to amusement, demand payment for the experience, and, as noted by Charles Moore in a famous article entitled You have to Pay for the Public Life, the element that seems to contribute most to Disneyland's success is the frank price-performance relationship .

A full price, however, that in return offers an impeccable service capable of solving any problem, responding fully to any questions and meeting any need concerning organization and the myriad possibilities of choice.

Baluba, Jean Tinguely, 1963-1964.

"Everything works, and in no way does it resemble the outside world. Life there is nothing like reality with all its imperfections. At Disneyland it's so much more real. Fountains sing, waterfalls flow, fireflies light up the trees at night, and everything is clean"[20].

So here not only is there everything we want but we are sure to find everything we want. We are confident that once we pay we will enjoy the excitement we are looking for and go home satisfied.

We face a reality that is more real than reality, that is, indeed, hyperreal: the simulation validates a tourist's expectations much more than its corresponding original. As had already occurred with the Universal Exhibitions that had taken place at the end of the 19th century, progress and technique are theatricalized, and spatial and temporal distances are cancelled through the reproduction of reality in scale: a simulation, a fiction of worlds, customs and atmospheres far from one another in space and time.

It is a bit like travelling in a sort of time-space machine that can shorten all geographical distance between us and other cultures and overturn the notion of time, eliminating all historical difference.

The iconography used in these interventions does not originate solely and exclusively in the Disney style but also reproduces bits and pieces of the history of architecture taken here and there. The deliberate effect of this concoction is that every image is easily recognizable and immediately identifiable. The appropriation of selected chunks of history is used on purpose for its scenic value. For example, the contemporary interpretation of the typology of the Grand Hotel rediscovers a taste for the spectacular, and especially for the marvelous, and constitutes a fantastic vacation from everyday life. These hotels function as great machines of hospitality that basically reproduce within them the same Disneyland philosophy [21].

They are designed so that visitors can savor different atmospheres, with rooms that are mini-apartments reproducing various themes, as is likewise the hotel's overall theme setting. Visitors are free to choose what sensations, locations and climatic features to have, almost in the same moment, almost in 'real time', to use a journalistic term.

Even the recreation of the atmosphere of historic European locales is often achieved by reproducing typical elements that are mixed together through the artificial creation of certain characteristic landscapes, despite the fact that all of it is fake and the very combinations of places are completely fictitious.

The overall structure of these complex sites is not built on the orthogonal pattern that is the basis of almost all American cities, but offers a Main Street which is always thought of as the backbone of a nucleus, to which all the other

Chapter 2

Bodys Isek Kingelez, Kimbembele Ihunga, Kimbéville 1993-94.

parts of the city are added – its squares, plazas and arcades; but right around the corner one meets up with more specific and characteristic places: a seaside setting, a lakeside landscape, a castle, or chugging up the Mississippi[22].

This potpourri of epochs and places gathers within itself all possibilities and choices, enabling the visitor to pursue imaginary trajectories in infinite combinations, weaving among them at will.

The phenomenon has been taken to such an extreme that the very experience of the new city being erected, called Epcot (Experimental Prototype Community of Tomorrow), created by Disney, which has recently gone beyond designing amusement parks to create actual cities, is organized primarily around two theme areas called Future World and World Showcase. The first features a future fantasy world, and the second displays snippets of history and urban sites, memories and landscapes of various countries[23].

An important component of this is the extreme stretching of truth. Disneyland makes it clear that its magic perimeter reproduces the truth by way of fantasy, in a world more real than real. Not only because it offers a concentration of excitement that it would take years of actual travel to approach, but also because it produces an exaggerated hyper-reality whose every feature is brought to excess in order to be more "true", to the point of near caricature.

What is interesting about cities is that they never fail to amaze us. What we see is always different and changed from what we expected to find. There is always the wonder of development, of change, of transformations, always different and unforeseen. But in Disneyland there is perhaps an opposite kind of amazement, for everything corresponds neatly to the stereotypes stored unconsciously by each of us about the characteristic features of the various countries of the world in their various epochs.

The Disney phenomenon, despite its design flaws and exaggerations, allows us, through concepts that seem near commonplaces, to identify certain traits that may be considered necessary, though not sufficient, for the creation of these spaces. Architectures must possess a narration. Disneyland, in its buildings, always tells a story which suggests that "buildings should never be boring, but should make people 'happy'"[24].

Expressing in architecture the magic of movies and not space as an extension of movies. Architecture must be able to express the fantasy, magic, dreams, and imagination that exist in movies.

Buildings must be interactive. Inside them we must be able to have experiences and emotions, and this should take place through the primacy of experience over intellect, or rather intellect should also be formed through a variety of experiences. As Alice enters the mirror, so entering Disneyland is like plunging into another world, and in that other world first of all the proportions are out of whack; experiences are distorted by a careful manipulation of proportions, shape, color and sound.

The Disney world is nothing but a paradoxical interpretation, an excessive response and perhaps a misleading solution to a real problem that has made itself felt increasingly in recent years. The lack of adequate public spaces and the indifference to the continual demands for leisure, entertainment and escapism that has been building up have resulted in an inability to understand the problem. And so the failure to grasp the problem and the inability to provide adequate answers have led to the expedient of appropriating the reality of the Disney cartoon world.

In the Disney world everything is too transparent, too equivalent to a slavish copy of a collective imagination, with no deviation or invention. Among other difficulties there is the great one of exporting all over the world a model designed for American society, which recognizes itself in it most naturally, so like itself, without making any changes.

The experiment near Paris of Euro-Disney is less successful because of the climate and because of the failure to take into account the existence of a purely European world of imagination and fable, which of course should have been introduced, even through a contamination with the world of Mickey Mouse.

All-Star Sports Disney World, Marne-la-Vallée-Chessy, Parigi.

Chapter 2

56

NOTES

1 Vattimo 1989.
2 See the writings of Wilhelm Dilthey, collected and translated into Italian in: Rossi, P. (ed.), *Critica della ragione storica*, Einaudi, Turin1954.
3 Foucault 1985.
4 See: Bloch, E., *Spirito dell'Utopia*, La Nuova Italia, Florence 1980.
5 "Kitsch, according to this logic, becomes an operation that still claims to count as an eternal monument, still affirming the stability and absolute perfection of the classical form of art". Vattimo1989, p. 98.
6 Lash 1990.
7 Baudrillard 1994.
8 Eco 1986.
9 Benjamin 1955.
10 "A work is foundation only to the extent that it produces a continuous effect of disorientation, never reassemblable into a final Geborgenheit. A work of art is never reassuring, 'beautiful' in the sense of a perfect reconciliation of inner and outer, essence and existence, and so on. It may perhaps have something of an Aristotelian catharsis, but only if the catharsis is understood as an exercise in subtlety, a recognition of the insuperable, earthly limits of human existence; not as perfect purification, but as phrònesis. It is in this sense not so much founding as unfounding that Heidegger's Stoss can be interpreted as analogous to the shock Benjamin speaks of". Vattimo 1989, p. 74.
11 Heidegger 1954.
12 Debord 1971.
13 "Neo-eclecticism and neo-romanticism are nothing but inadequate formulations of these critical trends, of which the former seems to look at the present, and the latter at the past". Perniola, 1990, p. 89; "A thought which Marc Augé provides many interesting examples of in non-European cultures, almost all based on processes of inversion, mimicry, and cancellation, which reveal in the work an esprit de finesse that seems to have disappeared from our culture". Perniola 1990, p. 64.
14 "The use of rubber and plastic materials that look like candy, and candy that looks like plastic, the level of edibility, or rather a visual edibility, a process that leads to 'an internalization of the artificial world begins with the moment of its seeming digestibility'"; Branzi 1996, p. 58.
15 "Since the most obvious result of the process of industrialization is the production of chaos and contradiction, the existence of multiple languages, the appearance of many different kinds of behavior, and the onset of various methods, we tend to work on a 'theory' of complexity and contradiction by introducing a different and imperfect modernity: a modernity in continuous development, full of elements of an irrationality that is alert to the dreams and emotions that are part of everyone's life and of Western culture". Branzi 1995, p . 117.
16 "What is this experience? It goes in an opposite direction from subjectivity. But this approach does not imply a movement towards objectivity. It is much more enigmatic. We have the increasing impression that between man and things there has been a process of mutual osmosis by which the former has become similar to the latter and, vice versa, the latter have taken on increasingly human features. This dual transference no longer concerns just the category of knowledge and action, as that of feeling, in the vastness of its exceptions, from sensitivity to emotivity, from listening to emotion". Perniola 1994, p. 52.
17 Taken from an interview with Walt Disney.
18 "A former Disney employee tells us: 'Walt's imagination ran like an engine at full throttle [...] you know how he got the idea for Disneyland? One day he put his granddaughter on a merry-go-round with wooden horses. While the kid went around on it he sat waiting on a park bench, munching peanuts. He reflected on a place where parents and children could have fun together [...] In short, by the end of the ride the idea was born and was realized in 1955, in an orange grove about twenty miles from L.A.: Disneyland, the first amusement park designed as an optical illusion.' Even in this case, his return to the origins was a condition of success, his return to the old merry-go-round with wooden horses, with little knights sticking rings on their toy lances, false deafening absences in which each of us becomes the passenger of a large fenakistiscope, the predecessor of the cartoons. Subsequently, it will be Disney World and the disciple of Méliès stretches his cinematic power even more over the world's appearances, organizing the city the way his predecessor tricked out his films. His former employee adds that 'the impact of Disneyland and Disney World comes from Walt's cinematic savoir-faire (illusion). His ideas don't compete but complement and prolong each other. The pedestrian is so happy in our realm because the volume of construction and means of transport is reduced to a fifth of its normal volume. Nothing, neither the trains nor the carefully reproduced cars are at normal scale, which generates [...] the dream'. Anyone walking here is like Renoir in his wheelchair that functioned as a movie camera, while the anamorphism is generated by an alteration of size, a falsification of the factors of distance and appearance". Virilio 1989, p. 54-55.
19 Von Moss 1996.
20 Moore 1965.
21 "A common feature of the Disney parks, over the years flanked by theme hotel complexes and office buildings designed by

internationally famous architects invited to interpret and participate in the Disney atmosphere, is their independent character; a kind of 'foundation places' rooted paradoxically in the absence of any place of reference, and precisely for this reason repeatable and reproducible in every part of the world, not to speak of the universe. In the meaning given to the term by Michel Foucault, we could classify the great Disney parks in the family of heterotopias, 'a kind of place outside of all places, yet effectively localized', or, more specifically, in the 'heterotopias of compensation', in the sense that the bond that these other places, built by Disney and the famous Disney Imagineering, have in relation to the remaining space a function that takes place between two extremes. On the one hand, they perform the task of creating a space of illusion that one denounces as more illusory than any real space, all the placements within which life is fragmented. On the other hand, they have the function of forming another space, another real space, likewise perfect, meticulous and well-organized, as ours is messy, ill-conceived and sketchy. We are all irresistibly attracted by ancient cities, whether real or plastic, especially if they have been able to ban automobiles. Walt Disney World has never allowed these monsters to breach its walls; the only surface vehicles authorized to circulate are those that are part of the choreography: steam locomotives, model trains, etc.",Vercelloni 1996, p. 35.

22 "The transition from signs to scenic design reflects an evolution from Vaughan Cannon to Walt Disney. A Disneyland Boulevard offers the pedestrian a three-dimensional theatrical-type of experience, with an iconography that evokes role-play: roguish pirates of the Caribbean or gladiators carousing in the Pompeii market. It is worlds away from the Cannon Strip's iconography, focused on the automobile. The change somehow implies gentrification. The iconography now does not insist so much on sin or vulgarity made reassuring and decorative, as it does on a wholesome family environment in its immediate references, albeit bizarre in its final effects. Which favors market expansion and increased profits. But will its wholesome scenery end up in good taste blandly homogenized and boring as only heaven can be?". Venturi 1996, p.10.

23 Epcot Center is an acronym which stands for "Experimental Prototype City of Tomorrow", which transforms the Disney dream into reality: "the construction of a twenty-first century citadel where, by wedding science with imagination, it is possible to live in harmony with technological advancement. The center is divided into two different theme areas, Future World and World Showcase. (...) Imagine a journey through time that will bring you from the dawn of Cro-Magnon man to a future dominated by the labyrinths of computer circuitry; bumping into incredibly realistic prehistoric animals in a building as big as three football fields, run entirely on solar energy; visiting a 21st century space colony and a town floating in the middle of the ocean; or experiencing the sensations of the different climates of a tropical greenhouse, or an arid desert swept by the fiery ghibli, or a snow-covered steppe (...) all on the same fabulous trip". Tosetto 1986, pp. 33-47.

24 Dunlop 1996.

Chapter 2

3 A city within the city

> **In Split the home of an emperor becomes a city for 3,000 people (...); what were once parts of the palace structure now serve as walls for dwellings. The niches are now rooms, the halls of the palace apartments, and everywhere there are recognizable fragments recalling the structure's original purpose. This enormous building, completely absorbed by the surrounding city, has demonstrated its ability to serve a new and different purpose, while the city has shown itself capable of adapting perfectly to its form. What we observe is a metamorphosis: the original structure is still present but the way in which antiquity has been swallowed up by contemporaneity makes one wonder what would become of the structure if it were emptied of its subsequent contents.**

(J. Bakema)

The Cosmopolis of the future, 1908.

A city within the city

The new public places, on account of their complexity, multi-functionality, variety and articulation, and on account of their hypothetical cultural force in the sense of production, circulation and exchange of culture, events and spectacles, can become, in particular urban situations, small authentic portions of alternative cities, can bring about modifications of the surroundings, and are in a certain sense phases of requalification and promoters of energy[1].

In general, a city's public places tend to reproduce spatial sensations of the older city and are based on a simulation of its historic urban pattern, reproducing to some extent its structure with the grid of main and side streets, squares, intersections, monuments and repeated elements[2]. There is an attempt to recreate the diversity and multiplicity of opportunities and experiences that the city seems to offer spontaneously.

They are simulations of familiar urban situations, of ancient cities, historic centers, recreating those environments on a human scale. Although collocated in a single space, whether a large roof or a large container, they try to reconstruct spatial and visual situations on a human scale, a landscape of echoes where people, even if they have changed their habits, must be able to control and manage space. Therefore, these complexes do not wish to be part of the city but rather its equivalent, almost its substitute. For the number and complexity of services they offer, they no longer need the city, but compete with it, represent it, empty it of meaning or, better yet, are themselves the city[3].

All of this occurs because the contemporary city, increasingly fragmented, begins to feel nostalgia for a restricted use of the city and its surroundings, for close relationships with one's peers, for squares, streets, parks, meaningful spaces between things, in order to be useful to the local inhabitants, as places and occasions for meeting, hanging out and being together.

"The imagery of modernity was full of metropolitan areas that could be traversed in a hurry, but the contemporary imagination has given renewed importance to plazas, side streets, 'slower' places that can become customary."[4]

In most of these places, the inner space mimics the outer one of the old city, especially the medieval parts: a strip of small shops runs along a narrow street which, in turn, leads to a square, a warren of streets and squares in double, triple height that attempt to recreate meaningful relationships between the different levels; place names evocative of urban spaces indirectly imagined and known.

The new public spaces posit themselves in relation to the city as great islands of aggregation that replace squares and streets in an urban context whose spaces are physically dilated, made up of streets and squares as in the ideal city of our imagination. They try to reproduce the city within them, and in some conscious or unconscious way want to gradually replace it.

What is it that enables these places to be considered micro-cities? First, the fact that there is a complexity of functions and uses, a multitude of the most varied activities for both leisure and activities of cultural and other types of exchange. Then the fact that they are easily accessible by car and public transportation. Finally, that they are in a circumscribed, identifiable, measurable place, perhaps, even with a little imagination, perceivable in all their complexity.

What must also be considered is the fact that the places themselves appear as defended, protected spaces transmitting a sense of security, just like the ancient cities with their well-defined perimeters, protected by defensive walls. These circumstances lead us into a world where we can abandon our fears, anxieties, cautions, the constant mental state in a contemporary metropolis,

Geodesic dome over midtown Manhattan, R. Buckminster Fuller, New York, 1968.

and therefore we are ready to relax and let ourselves go emotionally. Our minds are freer to open up, daydream, play. At this point too our reticence to consume relaxes, and we are more willing to spend our money.

This is also favored by the well-being we feel in our protection from air pollution and our insulation against noise, the weather and the external environment in general. We are, in short, in a kind of refuge[5]. These areas are at times closed, and at times, in more complex instances, have both open areas of greenery for outdoor activities, and closed, climatically controlled inner areas.

The landscape inside these places confers on the inhabitants of the outskirts the tacit advantage of a surrogate urban world. The absence of social life that is often a negative feature of the city streets can, in these air-conditioned, protected enclosures, be relieved by shopping, an activity that has become far more complex than the simple purchase of consumer goods. Shopping, a pastime that lasts on average several hours, may combine social gatherings,

Reconstruction of Diocletian's Palace in Split (E. Hébrard, 1908).

Chapter 3

courtship rituals, recreation, entertainment, education, care for children and the elderly, the exchange of products, and much more.

"Thanks to this new combining of multiple social activities, 'these places' become a serious alternative to urban street life, and this has become unintentionally an ideological fact" [6].

In any case, in the new public places there is always an artificial world that generally offers through naturalistic elements the man-nature relationship that has always characterized the urban format, with tree-lined boulevards, parks and fountains. Water too is often used, especially because it can suggest situations and images of bucolic tranquillity, at times accompanied by the evocative sound of water as in an Islamic garden. There is thus the introduction of authentically natural elements, besides artificial ones, through the sensory employment of representative smells and sounds.

There is also a series of measures in the use of light, such as large windows in both the roof and the façade, all designed to convey the sense of being outdoors [7]. It is a spatial situation that tries to recreate the setting of an ancient city, a situation on a human scale with familiar spatial relationships, in which people feel comfortable and which they relate to in an easy, spontaneous way. It substitutes the city, a surrogate for the urban world. The visitor finds a world of relations of proximity and vista: in short, an identity he knows.

These new, extremely complex centers are often an allegory of the city. Not of one city, but of all imaginable and unimaginable cities. They try to recreate an actual city, connoting it with all the features and quirks of such places, thus becoming a kind of urban concentrate. Almost a metaphor of the city, or a city made up of parts of other cities, an analogous city [8]; shaped not from a collage of landmarks but from the dreams and fantasies that every city possesses [9]. Already Benjamin, in speaking of the Parisian passages, defined them as hidden cities, like a closed world in miniature, ostensibly devoted to trade but really an important pole of attraction, a social gathering place, a hidden patchwork of public spaces dug into the city and resembling typical images seen in dreams.

"These galleries, a recent invention of industrial luxury, are glass-covered corridors with walls of inlaid marble, which stretch for whole blocks, whose owners have joined together for these speculations. On both sides of these corridors, which receive daylight from above, there are rows of the most elegant shops, so that this kind of passage becomes a city unto itself, indeed a world in miniature [10]."

It is a small truth, a portion of the truth, which can be one among many, rewritten many times within the same metropolis. A little like the ideal, fantasy vision of ancient Rome designed by Piranesi in his Campus Martius, where each

blueprint organism is in itself so complex as to seem the layout of the utopian cities of the sixteenth century [11]. A city made up of many fragments of cities randomly connected to each other, defined and recognizable urban units that are almost self-sufficient islands in a magmatic and random reality [12].

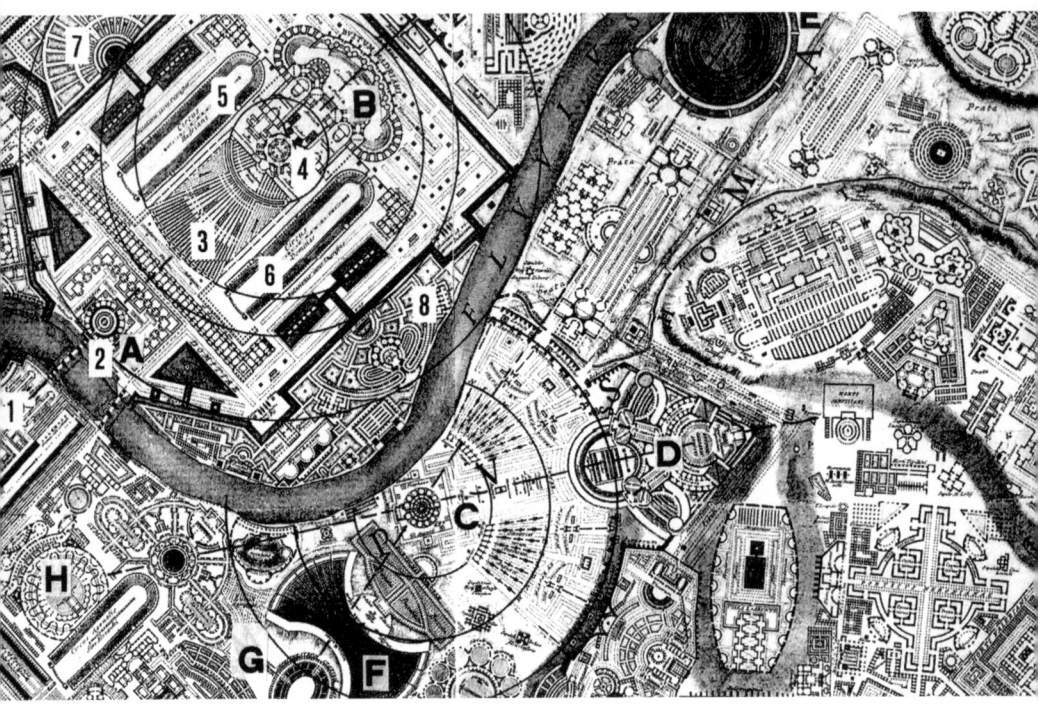

Campo Marzio, G. Piranesi, 1762.

Beyond all typologies

Public spaces that have many functions, often none of which predominates over the others, also pose a problem of surmounting the notion of architectural type.

They are simultaneously cultural centers, shopping malls, convention and conference centers, cinemas, theaters, museums, galleries, restaurants, bars, sports and entertainment facilities, and much more, and all of these together. They are fluid spaces, organized on several functional levels; flexible spaces that are constantly changing their purpose from one day to the next, and often within the same day. They are spaces characterized by a high degree of freedom, by infinitely differentiated aggregations, and by vast dimensions which can accommodate a myriad of events in a single enclosure.

They are lively places that, while markedly kitsch, can offer alternative spaces that teach us new rules for inhabiting them and moving within them [13].

They are places that belong to several building types and do not identify with just one. The very notion of type becomes obsolete in a culture that no longer recognizes itself in unitary, totalizing concepts but is linked to an episodic system that has taken on a de-totalizing, fragmentary character, denoted also by a certain randomness. These architectural styles force us to resort to the idea of typological desuetude, since they no longer seem to interpret the notion of type as a "scheme that can give rise to different configurations reflecting not only the dynamics of variation and interpretation but also the existence of a plan of negotiation about the position of the architectural product in the urban setting and its relationship with the adjoining buildings"[14].

They go further, imagining a fusion of types generating a metamorphic principle capable of endowing architecture with a greater degree of freedom and a myriad of extra possibilities. The extremely wide range of events that these places can accommodate is indicative of the staggering potential that can be experienced.

The notion of typology therefore loses its generalizing character of taking charge of society's representative intentions and must be able to "interpret the most captivating imagery resources of the metropolis". They can propose new rules to live by, new modes to follow, indicate new aesthetic directions, setting new styles of behavior and new uses, and suggesting the possibility of new relationships and connections.

It is a fairly common opinion in contemporary culture that type as such presents itself as a cognitive process through which the reality of architecture reveals its essential content and, at the same time, as an operational method that forms the basis of the very act of planning.

The very concept of typology must also be able to decipher the needs of the contemporary city. These places demonstrate the obsolescence of the definition of type, since their transformation lies in the wide range of freedom they make possible. The typology issue, which must be reckoned with, whatever its formulation, is an essential part of architecture, and with regard to these centers it can almost be defined by the term beyond-typology.

The new centers refer to the notion of typology as the transformation and interpretation of new modalities, although their condition neither denies nor rejects it but goes beyond it through an intensification of its features.

In a process of breakdown, the single elements themselves which make up the type are led back increasingly to the idea of archetype and tend to become autonomous elements with a life of their own: the great atrium, the gallery, the garret, the living area of the wall, the tall portico. All the elements which derive different typologies or that characterize them, once broken down, become autonomous units (often coinciding precisely with archetypal forms), having a life of their own and can be reassembled freely in myriad ways: assimilated,

La Ville Spatiale, Y. Friedman, 1958-1962.

superimposed, linked together ad libitum, according to the configurations desired, in a continuous unit-fragment link.

The beyond-typology concept points to the establishment in the design process of the new public places of "a metaphorical principle capable of giving to writing an iridescent, indeterminate" character: beyond-typology, therefore multiple affinity of an architectural product to various architectural styles.

The term beyond-typology suggests and interprets the dynamic character of the very notion of type, preserving the value of its evolution and power of transformation and not decreeing its ultimate demise.

Another feature of this new way of conceiving typology leads us to consider too, in an upside-down way, the process of identity formation. The new public centers no longer belong to functionalist thought, which rigidly separated all functions. Their desire is rather to integrate different uses and activities, as was customary in the pre-modern city. This occurs no longer within their core, from a preordained typological blueprint, but finds new vigor in its renewed relationship with the outside world, which defines identity by interpreting context. Increasingly, the "functional and representative content" of an architectural product or a complex of places, no longer comes from the typological blueprint structure but from the set of contextual elements, signs and traces that require continual interpretation. The Les Halles center, for example, appeared as a great hole in the center of Paris, a huge cavity formed in the city center, where the idea of a partially underground, labyrinthine, hidden world drew its origin from its wounded condition itself, a gash in the bowels of the earth formed by the demolition of the old 19th-century market structure. Likewise I. M. Pei's Louvre project, which appeared as a borderline condition whose purpose was to satisfy the museum's need for enlargement and to enhance the archaeological remains of the ancient fortress, but which found its autonomy in the extreme condition of an underground foundation in the heart of Paris.

Yet again, the idea of reproducing the shape of a hill for the new Saitama center in Japan, designed by Renzo Piano, was inspired by the undulating landscape. The birth and form of this great public center resulted from an altogether original interpretation of the hilly Japanese context.

Large interiors have become a constant in these centers, derived from the spatial concept of an identifiable place, protected by a boundary. They prove that the complexity and articulation of a city can be enclosed in an interior, which expands its domain by means of a real transfer of public space to its internal space [15].

The capture of the city, as Benevolo calls it, occurs through the reproposal of external portions, which almost reproduces an artificial universe in a large,

Les galeries de bois, Parigi, 1825.

Chapter 3

absolutely disproportionate space. One of the features of these vast interiors is the presence of a fluid space which is an empty space that contains everything but that can constantly change along with the events that take place inside it. Above all, it can change shape in relation to experiences, with still greater force than an empty urban space of streets, squares, agoras, forums. These large interior spaces seem characterized by an endless spatial play which in turn conceals other spatialities, where, almost in a Chinese box effect, these architectures can include objects within objects, spaces within spaces.

This topic calls for an analysis of the features that denote the typological research of these spaces, features that can be identified as: acceleration, as an experience that brings them to their limit; hybridization, as a contamination of several typological matrices; narrative, as the possibility of incorporating within it fragments of previous statutory definitions, "restoring to architecture the capacity of architectural products to be specified also in a literary sense"; topology, as a renewed contextual relationship.[16]

Acceleration

The acceleration factor introduces the temporal element in determining types, as an experience that invariably brings to its limit any attempt to define these spaces.

Acceleration is a particular condition that condenses several phases into one and instills a desire to experience several situations with greater intensity. One of the features that seem important for the new public places is the capacity to bring together many different situations at all levels of need that can be expected from these places, and to be able to experience them at close range and almost, to use a paradox, all together[17].

The experiences people once had in the course of a day were separate and well distinct from one another; each place had its own specificity, which was identified in a place appointed to this purpose and which provided a range of experiences that were secondary to its main function.

The acceleration we must contend with on a daily basis in today's world imposes constant, abrupt shifts of pace that force us to do several things together, even in our leisure time[18]. This is why it is important to find a place that can combine all our needs and satisfy all our desires without having us waste time. We often need everything at once and right at our fingertips.

The new public places, through their organization, must interpret this desire for speed, but how can they accomplish this? It is reasonable to assume that this can be done through the concentration and variability of their organizational essence as a public place.

There is need for a change in the way we conceive the architecture of new public places, or a way to accelerate their features and peculiarities, highlighting certain concepts, calling into question their status, their being. The acceleration of emotions, experience, ways of living, and the condensation of space and time mean that these places must somehow be interpreted by multiple forms of speed that characterize our daily lives.

Acceleration can also be understood in an emotional sense, the pushing of our experiences to their limit, the full, intense living of them to the point of

Las Arenas, shopping mall, Rogers Stirk Harbour + Partners, Barcelona, 2011.

dream and fantasy. Acceleration leads to the need to condense into a single container all the experiences, emotions and activities that were once carried out separately. To repeat, in the past each place had its own specific function, or at least a prevalent activity to which people attributed a distinct value, a fixed amount of time, and a well-defined pace and habit. All of this has been turned on its head in contemporary society, continually called into question, made unpredictable, and in any case subject to constant variability. The new centers must be able to handle several functions simultaneously or in rapid succession.

The mutation of space which occurs in these places causes, as Jameson says, loss of "the ability to orient the human body, to perceptually organize things immediately around it and to cognitively map its location in the outside world"[19]. The alarming point of separation between the body and the constructed environment around it is a symbol of our incapacity, at least for now, to fully understand the potentiality of these spaces.

Jameson, in describing one of the achievements of the architect Portman, suggests that we are dealing with a space, one of whose most exciting, enthralling features is that of enabling people to let themselves go, give up their sense of direction and knowledge of where they are.

L'empire des gares, D. Appia, 1978.

Narration

The experiential process of following a story, like that of walkng through a structured space, is, according to Bettetini, a process of identity construction, and this occurs in two ways. In terms of structure, texture, articulation of space, the subject is guided through a network of choices through which he assembles his own inner narrative, i.e., a story of responsibly absolved options. In terms of viewpoint, of spatial and narrative perspectives, the subject is invited to identify himself with and to distance himself from certain roles; to inhabit and abandon textual presences in a game of near and far, of self-discovery through a relationship with another than oneself, in an alternating play of empathy and exotopia [TN: the condition of finding yourself outside of yourself].

The narrative itinerary of a story, as of a work of architecture, refers to the basic idea of dynamic entity, constantly growing, constantly searching. A subject who inhabits structures that cannot fully define his itinerary but just stimulate his ongoing progress[20].

The Grand Roof Festival plaza, K. Tange, Osaka Expo, 1970.

The capacity of contemporary places must lie, according to Ricoeur, in knowing how to interpret space, prefigure stories, tell stories, enable human thought to roam through an imaginary time, a time that is rarefied or condensed by our imagination. Just as in contemporary literature, a story that is open, in which cultural hybridizations are interwoven, in which there are many beginnings and an interpretable ending; just as in contemporary novels, which almost take on the form of an encyclopedia, an open encyclopedia which enables us to weave together all the different disciplines and codes in a pluralistic, multi-faceted vision of the world[21].

As Calvino says, "the modern books we love most are born from the merging and clashing of a variety of interpretive methods, ways of thinking, styles of expression"[22]. In this sense, designed space, architecture, and therefore the types of spatial definition, may have similarities with narrative structure. Space in these places, precisely because of its richer and certainly different quality, because of the clairvoyant properties it must take on in the future, because of its capacity to be the seismograph of a future situation, can contain a pathos

and perhaps also an open-endedness like those of fiction, which, precisely because of its status of not requiring the immediate materialization of an idea, could be very helpful to us. For this purpose we could employ the analysis grid Paul Ricoeur proposes in his essay Temps et Récit, divided into the three successive phases of prefiguration, configuration and refiguration.

"For each of these phases, I ask myself what has become of the gap between literary narrative and architecture. My working hypothesis is that the gap gets reduced from one phase to another, so that at the point of refiguration the exchange between the spatiality of the narrative and the temporality of the architectural project is complete"[23].

It is at the level of literary narrative that the act of storytelling gets disengaged from the context of action. And it is precisely the autonomy of the narrative, with respect to the plot's action, that can offer hints and reflections, summon new meanings and help to interpret the architectural design.

First, the story is often a creation of meaning, a semantic innovation, and this happens whenever, for example, some heritage of the past is not only reutilized but also reinterpreted. The plot is derived from what Aristotle called mythos, a definition that stresses four aspects: a synthesis of heterogeneous elements with the various events in a story; the transition from an initial state to a final state through regulated transformations; the succession of vicissitudes that vitiate the work of correlation represented by the plot; the circular relationship between the whole and its parts.

Ricoeur argues that "interpreting the configuration of time through a literary story is a good exercise for interpreting the configuration of space through an architectural design. Between the two 'poetic' actions there exists much more than a simple parallelism; we recognize the existence of the architectural design's temporal, narrative dimension. On the horizon of Investigation there is, as has frequently been suggested, the manifestation of a space-time in which narrative values and architectural values are exchanged". As in a narrative plot there is a synthesis of heterogeneous elements, so architectural works, and in this case public places, constitute a polyphonic message that can be read in an incorporating or analytical way, and, qua plot, does not muster together just events but "points of view, in the form of reasons, causes, coincidences". The reciprocity between the whole and the part and the hermeneutic circularity of interpretation that results, has an exact correspondence in the mutual implications of architectural components. In fact, as Paul Ricoeur goes on to

La *Città analoga*, Aldo Rossi, 1976.

state, architecture and narrative have pursued similar historic paths, and it is at the point of refiguration that they exchange their meaning in new possibilities of inhabiting the world, which emanate together from the art of storytelling and the art of constructing.

Narrated time and constructed space exchange their meanings. Understanding a text and a place through the active role of the reader can reveal what is hidden and transform what is. It is very interesting to think of a city as a text, that is as a receptive and active inhabiting that implies a careful rereading of the urban environment, a new apprenticeship in the juxtaposition of styles, and therefore also in stories about life, of which all monuments and buildings seek a trace.

A reader of narrative does not perceive just the sense of a narrated story but the world projected in the text, which is his real world offered up to interpretation, or to revelation and transformation.

To conclude, the architecture of these places, through the spatial telling of stories, which are its hidden matrix, can stimulate and suggest to the reader of architecture his own real world, his own baggage of experiences, sensations and especially knowledge, which through further spatial, visual and emotional experience can be crucial and formative in the different ways of experiencing these spaces, these worlds, and in his capacity to know how to interpret them.

"The tension between an experience of purely cognitive appreciation and a more complex and articulate experience defines the transition from the interpretive paradigm to the experiential one"[24].

Consider the experience of appreciating a story as a complex, articulate experience, and consider it interfused with the subject's other life experiences, in precisely the same way that one can think of the concrete spatial paths offered up to the subject's practical experience; his spatial path, understood as the possibility of transforming space into a story, or into a place where there is a possible quest for identity.

A great container

The problem and the questions posed by hyperspaces (if we may so call them) arise from the fact that we are losing a way to interpret them, manage them, and above all we are losing the perceptual experience for relating and harmonizing with them, precisely because our systems were formed on other types of spatiality.

Since they are spaces characterized mainly by heightened degrees of freedom and a collage of differences, they are characterized by bigness and can accommodate a proliferation of events in a single container[25].

The container, as something that can encompass multiple meanings, languages, races, autonomies and expressions, can accommodate it all inside: all the various expressions of the contemporary world, and then interpret society's numerous variants and diversities. The container, like a contemporary novel, is an encyclopedia, a method of knowledge, a network connection among the world's facts, people, things. It is itself a world seen as a system of systems, in which every single set conditions the others and is conditioned in turn. There is a:"simultaneous presence of heterogeneous elements that combine to determine each event (...); the container is seen as a possible refuge for every single element, which seen as the hub of a network of relationships, able to multiply its relationships in such a way that its descriptions and digressions become infinite"[26].

This is after all what occurs in architecture itself, since it is the only art that contains, "that gives room to whatever comes by", as Gadamer says, emphasizing the relationship between architecture and the other arts.

"Architecture encompasses all the other forms of representation, all the expressions of the figurative arts and ornamental forms, and provides sites for performances of poetry, music, mime and dance (...). (In including and providing room) architecture is never neutral, imposing, in general, its point of view (or proposing) an interpretation that suggests how the inner and the outer is to be configured. (After all, it is an attempt to communicate, even to seduce, which is expressed by generating) a sense of decorum, or rather by creating and decorating the tray that sustains the other arts"[27].

The container is a tray, a place that is easily identified by its capacity to define a limit, to protect, shelter, define boundaries, and that on its inside can possess an autonomy of expressions and meanings. The very term "container" suggests that it differs from its content, or rather, that it can receive within it a variety of contents, also quite different among them.

It is a big object which, in relating to the city with its presence, leaves its inside open to the most varied interpretations. It is just a big roof under which an entire city grows and blossoms, which opens a shelter against the unknown and the infinite; it is in some way directly connected to the idea of city walls which in the past, in addition to being an actual physical urban limit, was an element that defined what was outside and what was inside. Speaking of a container, one cannot fail to relate to the idea of a big inside and to try to understand why that inside is increasing its domain and taking on such decisive importance in the urban structure. All this comes about because the outside has changed its identity; it used to present itself with well-defined spaces, such as streets, squares, monuments; it was a living tissue that changed over time but that always respected certain relationships, such as full-empty, neighborhood and city, downtown and outskirts, city and countryside, private and public. Now the city lacks these nice distinctions. In the absence of a collective project, and therefore of what the outside world meant for the city, namely memory, symbol, collective identity, the inside is the only chance, the only meaningful, manageable dimension that offers a possible and desirable mixture of different uses and a variety of activities, giving a final blow to the idea of a mono-functional city, organized according to the obsolete division by functions.

If we look at the history of architecture we find examples of interpretations of the container concept, a certain something that contains something else and that is not immediately attributable to the urban experience in that given historical period.

The Roman baths are certainly one of the earliest and most interesting examples of a multi-function container which played a major role in the structure and development of the city. In these great ancient Roman complexes we see quite clearly the more salient and qualifying features of a way of experiencing the city and especially of employing the leisure time of Roman civilization.

During the Renaissance too certain architectural works seemed like foreign objects plopped in the heart of the medieval cities, asserting themselves mainly through two provocative stances: the great Renaissance palaces, on the one hand, breaking with tradition by introducing into the fabric of the medieval city new additions, posited according to other rules; and on the other, imposing themselves with a language that had universal aspirations, in clear conflict with local traditions.

In the mid-nineteenth century another object, rather alien to the culture of the time, rose up bearing certain features that helped define the container idea: the Crystal Palace.

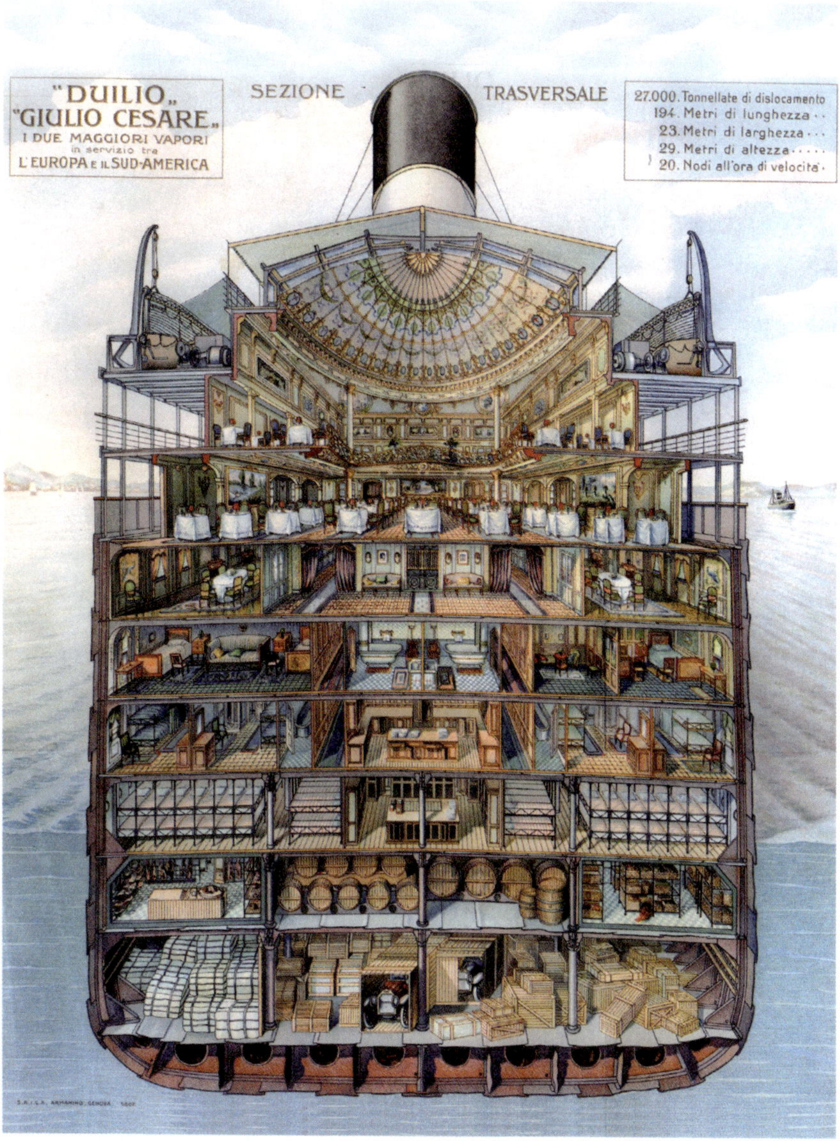

Section of ships *Duilio* and *Giulio Cesare*.

The interest in the birth and development of this building was due to the invention of a light structure that upset the concept of typological organization, architectural materiality and functional stiffness[28]. The building was the answer to two fundamental questions in the culture of that period: the search for a link between nature and technology, the greenhouse and the attempt to solve the problem of a commercial aesthetic and mass consumption at the moment of its sudden appearance.

"A large container, which through a shell that suggests levity, lightness and purity, its immense size, spurred expertly by the transparency of its surfaces, its creative force and its material competence expressed by its volume and individual details"[29].

It stands as an interesting antecedent of the modern complexes, comprising in its essence all the factors that will become crucial in defining our present-day containers. Benjamin expressed it this way: "the world expositions transfigured the exchange value of merchandise; they created an environment whose utilitarian value was of secondary importance; they inaugurated a phantasmagoria which mankind entered to let itself be distracted. The entertainment industry made this task easy by lifting it to the height of merchandise."

The Crystal Palace also had the great merit of provoking, because of its innovative features, a great sense of wonder and awe; a place for celebrating and displaying discoveries and transformations, making the best use of new materials by amplifying their properties and specific features, and where, as John Mc Kean notes, there was an attempt to reconcile "art and industry, production and research".

"Those who were lucky enough to see it did not know how to express the sense of wonder and even mystery that stirred within them (...) something that went beyond the capacity of discernment or imagination (...) one felt that it was something more than what one saw or was proposed."[30]

And yet, the experience of the Crystal Palace, with its almost mythological name, suggests another question of great timeliness and interest for future public centers: that it is important to invent a name for these centers and that they, by that name, are enriched with a further semantic attribute. For the first time ever the effect of assigning a catchy, imaginative name helped create a value independent from what at first sight seemed a "manufacture of weak identity"[31]. Thus for the first time in architecture it was the title of the object that counted, something Marcel Duchamp would later demonstrate with his works.

The last chronological element in the genealogical list of containers is the skyscraper, whose birth posed two problems for the new architecture: the

Chapter 3

principle of identification, and the relationship between inside and outside. From the start, skyscrapers have had to face the problem of differentiating themselves from other skyscrapers in the urban panorama. The issue of recognition became crucial, since the principle of individualization of the new commercial buildings was an integral part of their success. "In the skyscraper as totem the theme of the physiognomic juncture links with the search for a form, to create a stylistic dilemma"[32]. The skyscraper witnessed the start of a series of experiments that could take place thanks to the introduction of new elements, one of which was the elevator.

The elevator, this mechanical device that disrupted the traditional distribution of buildings, also radically changed the way in which their conditions for enjoyment were utilized.

Crystal Palace, J. Paxton, London Great Exhibition, 1851.

The introduction of a cinematic dimension in the perception of interior space owed itself primarily to the use of the elevator. The quick ascension one experienced in the cabin connecting all the floors, through the sequence of sprints through the different layers of a building, replaced in the blink of an eye its horizontal succession of spaces and multiplied its distributive and functional potential. From then on the commingling of different functions became more natural, no longer tied forcibly to a logical-distributive succession[33].

The relationship that the big containers had with the street is not only what was previously described as their perception in motion but was also what came about from their changed role qua street. This in fact has now become basically

Galeries Lafayette, J. Nouvel, Berlin, 1993-1996.

a tool for the high-speed flux, to the near disappearance of the multifunctional character that had been typical of it since antiquity. The street, as an element which enabled a multiplicity of situations to co-exist, tends to disappear or rather exist only physically, serving the exclusive function of a space for movement.

The big containers thus have the task of replacing the original role of the street as the urban space where all public events, demonstrations and encounters take place, and of drawing into their interior, under their protection, the development and growth of a new public space, since it is in these elements that we must polarize many of the aspects of the contemporary city. A great responsibility is at stake; much of the survival of the city must be entrusted to

Guggenheim Museum, F. L. Wright, New York, 1943.

the new complexes that have become a place for relating and encountering, activities whose natural setting was once streets and squares.

In these places we must create fictions and illusions and make sure that people do not just walk through but stop, feel the presence of others, feel part of a community and try to pause en masse, obstructing the law of fluid mechanics. "The private space of the home has been abandoned en masse to fill the public or semi- public space of pause".

The city needs the efficiency and the stimulus of movement as much as it needs pause and reflection, two segments that must be able to coexist like the sounds and pauses of music.

The big containers act as catalysts, whose vital purpose is to create in the city renewed areas for exchange, for the circulation of culture, and to investigate as much as possible the multiplicity of situations offered by the constant interactions among infinite diversities.

Autonomy of parts, unity of the "whole"

In his De re aedificatoria Leon Battista Alberti makes an analogy between home and state, maintaining that cities are like large homes and homes are like miniature cities. "If the city, in accordance with the opinions of philosophers, is actually a big house, and also, a house is a small town, why should we not consider in turn the individual parts of the house, such as galleries, arcades, rooms, courtyards, and so on, as little houses?"[34]

The parts of a whole, as Vittorio Ugo noted, are predominantly structural and formal elements that have a greater individual and formal autonomy, especially with respect to the configuration of the architectural object.

The relationship between the part and the whole is very complex and hardly reducible to a combinatorial technique, as occurs with simple components[35], as Alberti maintained. Moreover, Alberti's insight is quite relevant for the contemporary city, especially in relation to those large complexes, which contain so much more.

The part, therefore, indicates a precise configuration, historically concrete and endowed with a name: it is a classificatory, functional sectioning of the whole, just as names designate significant, autonomous parts of reality. Language sections, names, knows, articulates, connects, designs. The elements of architecture are all nameable, because names are a symptom of discovery, of a way to organize reality and of a new element placed on the market of linguistic production and exchange.

The relationship between the part and the whole is defined by the principle of analogy, which can be presented linguistically by the two rhetorical figures of metonymy and synecdoche. The latter indicates the part used to refer to the whole; and the former the possibility of using in the language of architecture a non-architectural word that offers to our eyes and minds features of problematic contiguity, so as to be able to transfer a term from the concept to which it applies to another with which it is in a relationship of dependence[36].

When the part is thought of as describing the whole, it is an important structural part which summarizes a broader concept that becomes a genetic principle. Single parts tend to become single architectures, tend to configure themselves as a type,

Escalator, archive image.

Le premier ascenseur, ville de Saint Denis, 1869.

to have a structural plan of their own, which organizes the form starting from an element assumed to be essential and privileged. The parts take on an autonomy and heterogeneity of their own; they can transform themselves autonomously, have a spatially independent meaning of their own, live independently, each evolving differently according to its distinct history and possibilities.

The unity of the whole concerns more the relationship with the city, while the autonomy and freedom of the parts concerns more the human scale. A good example is the 19th-century gallery as a great unifying element that must include independent elements within it, and where the balance between the parts and the whole is important. All the inner fronts were designed first and a single architectural character was imposed on the interior; now they were in a certain sense free, the façades themselves independent and the unifying element furnished solely by the roof.

Zeilgalerie *Les Facettes*, R. Kramm, Frankfurt, 1992.

And if it is true, as Koolhaas maintains, that great size seems to destroy what comes into contact with it, it is also true that it "puts back together what it breaks". As in a great cauldron (the ideology of the American Melting Pot, a crucible in which different nationalities creeds, cultures and races simmer in coexistence), endless possibilities and relationships raised to the highest expression lead to the development of organizing strategies for independence and interdependence within a larger entity, in a symbiosis that enhances specificities rather than impair them, creating a kind of programmed alchemy, as in the design of all architectures that must accommodate several independent elements, where the important thing is the balance between the unity of the whole and the freedom of the parts[37]. The combination of independent parts and a whole can be achieved in several ways. On the one hand, through the process of combining different faiths, cultures, religions, creeds, philosophies and races that manage to live together because of the infinite possibility of addition and reaction with each other, so as to propose almost a model of controlled alchemy that somehow tolerates all varieties, even making them necessary in a logic of pluralistic views. This free interpretation of the parts is but a need in today's society for each individual to be represented by a small part, just as every other individual will be represented in another way.

On the other hand, there is the list methodology, like the dismemberment of an organism, where it is more difficult to control the unity of the whole, its harmony and meaning within a larger whole. A formal, functional unity is hard to achieve through a comprehensive, overall, rigid, total design in which all the variables are anticipated. By contrast, the individual units with autonomous capabilities make possible a much more flexible grid that permits multiple combinations. This is a method that effectively interprets the needs of a heterogeneous society, full of contradictions, differing, multiple desires, continual variables, a polyphony of life styles, which identifies more successfully the different clocks that Massimo Cacciari speaks of[38].

Fluid space is created between autonomous elements, a space determined within the large interior between one element and another; a space in which the various autonomous elements float and which becomes a unifying amalgam that allows a thousand trips and trajectories in all directions and thus preserves great flexibility as a "space between things".

Inside-outside, private-public

"The contrasts between inside and outside can be an important manifestation of architectural complexity. However, one of the most important dogmas of the twentieth century has been the need for continuity between them: the inside should be expressed on the outside"[39.]

Modern functionalist architecture created the need to provide continuity between outer space and inner space: the inside had to be readable on the outside. The continuous space used to link outer with inner space and the new possibilities offered by the new technologies and their rapid progress, mark the substantial difference from certain architectures of the past that also sought this kind of unity. "Modern architecture wants a building to develop from the inside outwards and wants the continuity and unity of all its spaces".

Buildings become more open, tending towards an absolute transparency that makes the inside seeable. Once it became possible to open great windows, interiors have nothing to hide, everything is perceived and revealed outside, and even when glass is not used as a mirror, the architecture of the outside must reveal, must provide a rereading of everything that is inside. The façade, the external view, does not lie, must not deceive; everything that lies behind it must be expressed toward the city.

Actually, the contrast that can be created between inside and outside can generate an interesting degree of architectural complexity, because whatever does not show through to the outside becomes startling, magical, since it manifests itself unexpectedly on the inside. The main purpose of the inside is to guarantee the articulation and fight the chaos of the city with its closed, gathered element, which protects from what is outside[40].

The ambiguity that is created in the contrast between inside and outside, between what is private and what is public, between the empty and the full, becomes a decisive factor in the formation of new public places.

The outside of these places must contain a complex inside, often rich and full of endless surprises, and must at the same time relate to the city, establish with it a relationship of continuity, discontinuity, break, adaptation. It therefore creates a contrast between inner and outer forces, and the architecture of these places necessarily generates elements of ambiguity, uncertainty. Its interest lies in being able to interpret them in different ways, in being able to discover them little by little, in being able to distinguish this ambiguity of what is outside from what is inside, with a sensation of continual discovery.

The Nolli Map of 1748, an expressive, strongly contrasted plan of the city of Rome, already identified as public places, besides its squares and streets, all the palace courtyards and the interiors of the more important churches and monuments. Through a continuous back and forth movement between indoor and outdoor places it highlighted a continuum of public spaces that in a careful present-day analysis seems an integral portion of these centers[41].

The fact of being continually inside interiors that, while private, are earmarked for collective use, and of walking through streets and squares that are wholly for public use, and private courtyards that can have a collective use, becomes a metaphor for the complexity of spaces and places that are created in these new public centers and for the continual loss of sense of direction that one experiences.

The possibility of being simultaneously inside or outside, since one can be inside a large interior but outside with respect to other architectural elements that are inside, or be inside an architecture that is in turn inside a big container, leads us to conclude that the concepts of inside-outside, private-public, are relative concepts more than opposing terms, which depend on various factors, such as the observer's standpoint: where one observes from and with respect to what[42].

When one speaks of inside-outside in the context of the new public meeting places, one cannot fail to refer to the passages, which originated in Paris as covered streets and in a short time became a new kind of very interesting urban public space, both for the new relationships that it created within a consolidated city, and for the kind of original space it brought about.

They were born to exploit the internal spaces between blocks, thus using leftover spaces of no value, and formed a network of covered walkways running through most of the city. Since they were protected from traffic and noise, they become places for meeting, strolling, shopping, doing business and making culture; in short, a new, extremely impressive public space; its special lighting from above through glass structures gave one the sensation of being in an interior and of losing all sense of being inside or outside[43].

The sense of ambiguity that these places convey is due to the relationship between their inner and outer spaces. Designed as an uninterrupted sequence, they became relative to the user and therefore to each other and one did not know if he was in an external public space or in an internal private one, so that even the notions of public and private became ambiguous, uncertain and confused.

The city therefore spawns a new way of using more hidden and remote spaces, like a worm that has slowly made its way by opening a breach hidden within the structure of the city, a maze that, in contrast to the square, which is a place to stay in, becomes a place to walk in, wander in, where one can lose himself, walking and losing his sense of direction and then finding himself he knows not where in the city[44].

This labyrinth of public spaces, excavating by subtraction in the urban structure authentic inner-outers, "opens up like a landscape and closes up as in a room". Their dual nature of being one thing while seeming another, this inner-outer, private-public, light-shadow, maze-room, familiar-unfamiliar, dream-reality ambiguity makes them into a very present-day kind of public space.

Benjamin writes that "(...) the most important buildings of the nineteenth century are the passages: houses and passage-ways that have no external façade, as the dream. The passages are like architectural dreams."

The Interior of St Peter's, G. P. Pannini, National Gallery, London 1742.

A musical Party, Pieter De Hooch, National Gallery London, 1677.

Royal Danish Playhouse (Skuespilhuset), Lundgaard & Tranberg Architects, Copenhagen, 2004.

Chapter 3

The passages, residual fragments corresponding to the splintering of the collective urban experience, which Franco Rella sees as characterizing the onset of metropolitan modernity, became precursor-places or rather an object of attentive reflection for the possible definitions of new public spaces in today's city.

We are faced with a new attitude; the word passage itself made clear the transitional nature, the idea of movement of this place, a way of communication, a space that developed within another building but from which it remained autonomous, with a different function.

Streets protected by glass, that became a building, animated to left and right by shops, which might also house workshops, offices and dwellings: a

Galleria BCE, S. Calatrava, Toronto, 1994, umbrella-like steel structure.

public space on private ground that permitted circulation, a space offering protection against bad weather, but also from pollution, and, finally, a space reserved exclusively for pedestrians. The great protagonist of the passage is man: "The passages are at the service of the public, which feels more at ease under the artificial light of the theater foyers, café terraces, big restaurants and bars, under the gallery glass, in this illusionist atmosphere, this man-made jungle, this reality under a bell-jar that replaces nature"[45].

Precisely because of their ability to see beyond, to react and so anticipate the needs and peculiarities of the new contemporary spaces, it seems appropriate to summarize the main features of these passages, some of which are similar in all respects to those of certain new cutting-edge public spaces:
- the gallery, the particular use of light, the magical accessibility to leftover spaces;
- the dreamlike, labyrinthine space, the taste for surprise;
- the internal reproduction of the street with materials, proportions and sensations of an external place, which however is internal;
- the ambiguity of a public space which resembles the livingroom of one's home;
- externally unrecognizable, the external image of the buildings involved is not affected;
- multi-activity use of space; the origin of a new public space not destined solely for purchasing but including many activities of the most varied kind.

Flexibility and its variations

Flexibility as a property or characteristic of adaptability, as the capacity to vary and change in accordance with different situations or conditions, can be understood, in the case of the big containers, in various ways, ranging from flexibility of use, to flexibility of interpretation, to flexibility of organization, and finally flexibility understood as an indispensable condition for becoming: a key requirement for an open design method.

The flexibility feature in the use of these places corresponds to their remarkable adaptability in performing different tasks, which may be contemporaneous or vary over time. The different purposes which these great centers are able to fulfill can be ordinary or extraordinary, typical of daytime or nighttime activities, and can vary from day to day or on a weekly or monthly basis. The flexibility of these places corresponds to their capacity to meet continually changing needs, and therefore to take on multiple aspects.

The ways of experiencing these spaces are almost endless and as we go through the phases of the day they change their appearance, thus changing their function. A good example of this is the *Maremagnum*, a multifunctional complex in Barcelona, located at the end of a pier of the old port. Its special feature is a large roof that opens up to become a vast terrace. During the day it serves as a mini-golf course, a bar with outdoor seating where you can take the sun, watch the sea while sipping a drink, or play a round of golf; by night it turns into a super-equipped discotheque with various dance floors for listening to different kinds of music, illuminated intermittently like a great lighthouse looming over the sea. What a few hours before was a quiet oasis of peace, sun and sea, turns into a crowd-packed place full of noise, dancing, excitement and fun; even the mini-golf course, with its green carpet lit up in a special way, contributes to the flamboyance of this fantastic, dreamlike, extravagant place.

The new centers feature flexibility in another sense too, in that they are not entirely passive but also active, where the user can interact in certain ways with the physical structure, causing certain changes, or make choices from among various options that lead to immediate but different results from one time to the next46. These places must of course be pre-contrived to contain variables that allow a limited degree of control.

All this to ensure that the user of these spaces feels at home and able to make use of forms of knowledge most congenial to him, liberating fantasies and games not always possible in congested everyday life.

There is also an aspect of flexibility in its organization: the potential derived from invention and the use of elevators and treadmills, devices that allow rapid and continuous access to the various levels, layers and hidden meanders of these places. These have greatly enriched the opportunity to explore, see and interpret never-before-seen spatialities. In this way architecture no longer has a "beginning and an end" and we can start where we want to make a contact; we can choose, and the elevator is a further factor of choice. The introduction of elevators allows vertical layering; the building can be quickly traversed both vertically and horizontally, without respecting the classical spatial hierarchy from bottom to top; sometimes these architectures are designed to be crossed inversely, from top to bottom, thus taking advantage of the building contrariwise, from the sky to the ground[47].

Elevators and escalators are defined as giant kinetic sculptures and make up much of the scenic effect and the fun the interiors of these new collective places have to offer. Walt Disney called them ironically people-movers[48]. These mechanical devices, emblems of movement, end up replacing the allegorical meanings of the architectural promenades of old. Our narrative pathway is thus highlighted by these machines of movement.

Flexibility must inhere in the design itself. As in literature the contemporary novel is not shut within a method but is born from the confluence of multiple interpretations, styles of expression, ways of thinking; so architecture must be able, over its skeletal structure, to allow for continual exceptions and unexpected situations. It is understood, thanks to a series of economic theories that identified it well before our discipline did, that in order to provide for a range of variables, unexpected events that are not readily calculable, the secret lies in not adopting a rigid, unitary, all-encompassing structure that tries to define everything and at once. The structure should be limited to basic definitions that posit the key points of intervention and allow over time the flux of ongoing change for a high degree of adaptability. In this way unforeseen changes, true variables, can be added without altering the original conception, on the contrary enriching it with new input and meanings[49].

Franco Rella in Metamorfosi writes: "The 'right' method is not therefore the most 'resistant' to reality but the most flexible, the one that is able to question itself, redefine itself, when some other formation succeeds in getting closer to the unknown reality"[50].

Flexibility, understood in this way, becomes the basic requirement for an open design method that is always ready to question itself and finds its pristine

force in starting over from scratch. It is important to have fixed, rigorous points, but the connection between them must be as evanescent as possible, enriching itself with new data and further opportunities, and therefore potential changes.

There is the difficulty of stabilizing these places in a fully formed vision, inserting them into a finite message, as in contemporary novels. Calvino cites, in this connection, two great 20th-century novelists, Musil and Gadda. But Proust's Recherche too is characterized by the impossibility of concluding: the reader cannot conceive of his encyclopedic novel having a plausible end.

Calvino maintains that the great challenge for literature is knowing how to weave together the different disciplines and codes into a pluralistic, multi-

Souterrain tram tunnel, OMA R. Koolhaas, Den Haag, 2005.

faceted vision of the world and how "(...) In our era literature has been taking on this ambition to represent the multiplicity of relationships, both under way and potential. Even if the general framework has been carefully designed, what matters is not its closing itself in a harmonious figure, but the centrifugal force that it unleashes, the plurality of languages as guarantee of a partial truth"[51].

Today we are faced with the formation of an open encyclopedia; a totality that is not potential, conjectural, pluralistic, is no longer thinkable: "(...) the modern books that we love are born from the merging and clashing of a variety of interpretive methods, ways of thinking, styles of expression."

Sir Joan Soane's museum, Cripta, J. M. Gandy, London, c. 1826.

103

Nucleus and shell

In the big containers the shell and the nucleus have separate lives. The one should no longer be thought of in function of the other, and there should no longer be a biunivocal correspondence between them. The outside and the inside are related to different worlds.

The shell, often on a large scale, is related to the city with a speed of perception which alters the very features of the building. It must therefore convey an image of immediacy in the heterogeneity of the city; in a landscape of disorder, fragmentation and dissociation, the great shell stands as an island, an archipelago of worlds in their own right.

In Piranesi's Campus Martius the city is fragmented into a magma of hermetic objects, and one cannot avoid being bewildered and awed in their disquieting presence[52].

They are great objects that relate to each other in a liquid space, no longer representing a single utopia but many heterotopias expressed in their various internal worlds. As in an encyclopedia the accesses to understanding are infinite, so these shells have a multiplicity of interpretive keys.

The nucleus, however, is a separate world that deals primarily with the variety of human needs, the multiplicity of human habits and the infinite possibilities of human demands[53]. The ambiguity and complexity of the relationship between shell and nucleus find in the building's skin its most conspicuous layer, the point of maximum contradiction. As a middle space, a place of transition that becomes architecture itself, the shell is an autonomous element that has a life of its own. Aldo Van Eyck has said: "Architecture should be thought of as a configuration of clearly defined intermediary places. This does not imply a continuous transition or an infinite postpositing as regards location and conditions, but a break with the contemporary concept (read: sickness) of spatial continuity and the tendency to cancel every articulation between spaces, as for example between inside and outside, between one space and another (between one reality and another). Instead, the transition should be articulated by means of definite 'middle' places that stimulate an immediate awareness of what is significant on the other side. In this sense, a 'middle' space is the common ground in which opposite polarities can once again become binary phenomena"[54].

In the relationship between nucleus and shell it may be that the façade is completely absorbed in the building's formal configuration. The intermediate element, as a place of transition between outside and inside, becomes the shell itself and is identified as a skin that enwraps something and encompasses all.

The Ark, R. Erskine, Hammersmith, London, 1992.

"The shell replaces the façade, cancels it out. In an attempt at formal configuration it is often the shells that tend to be the unitary representation of great objects, enfurled volumes"[55].

They become single volumes where it is difficult to identify the façade element when the parts are dismantled.

"These are no longer traditional buildings but volumes in search of a formal configuration. All this has shifted attention to the building's surface, which is no longer definable as a façade. Great volumes that are cut, folded, curved, rounded, a great skin that enwraps a set of other boxes".

The façade may maintain a certain autonomy, and its becoming 'a transitional place' can occur in various conformations: as a skin that has the function of a mechanism or filter, or as a screen, or a mere artifice.

The façade, as a transitional place, as an intermediate, threshold factor, becomes an element of mediation with the context, through which strategies of reseaming and redefinition can be implemented. The façade, as a freewheeling element, can interpret a new look by endowing a new role on the city's existing complexes, whose identities, it is felt, need to be rethought. Through a new, more attractive look and a new interpretation of the possibilities of use that can come forth with a change of identity, the solution to a series of technological and environmental problems can be dealt with in a single blow.

The façade, as an environmental filter mechanism, becomes an element of transition, since it absorbs both the outside and the inside, and by being in contact with the two worlds receives impulses and ideas from both. Thus it reacts differently according to the different situations that arise. The façade lives two completely different lives, has two sides that can condition it. It is actually a shell element that has acquired a life of its own, becoming a sort of architectural artefact itself, with mechanisms and rules of its own, independent from the rest. Once the façade has acquired its autonomy it becomes a mechanism that can move, having within it systems of aperture and closure, and breathe by sensing or eliminating light and temperature changes inside it. In short, it takes on in autonomous fashion the task of defining the very life of the building.

It may function as an environmental filter for weather control, as in Jean Nouvel's Arab World Institute building, where it regulates light-shade intensity and fine-tunes environmental factors. It becomes a filter capable of modifying the passage of light and images, an easily readable section filter, a self-representing threshold.

It is a space that absorbs both the outside and the inside. The skin is independent of the building context, a coating that becomes an element expressive in itself through the employment of artificial materials or natural materials used in a new and original way.

The concept of a building as a unitary organism has been lost, and has become instead mainly a sum of elements, whose parts have a certain autonomy and tendency to follow their own laws, specific rules and different functions, but above all a communicative capacity of its own. The façade, which is the building's image, aims at narrating or communicating something. This can happen in several ways. Thanks to the array of opportunities a façade can utilize, to our greater technological knowledge, to the increasingly sophisticated techniques of communication with liquid crystal, to a new expressiveness of materials, continuously enriched by contributions from other disciplines, the opportunity itself provided by the reinterpretation of traditional materials, and, lastly, to the ability to acquire its own physical space, its detached, habitable depth.

The outer skin has lost its biunivocalness with the interior and acquired an interesting autonomy, which enables it to relate, as we have said, to both the inner and the outer reality, thus incorporating and absorbing the two different expressions.

The change in its relationship with the outside world is concretized in its ability to take in ideas and suggestions and incorporate everything that lies in the outside world. The shell, no longer existing soley for the spatial and distributive organization of the interior, dialogues with the opportunities the place provides. It becomes an active element that can change continually and communicate a variety of messages and signals interpretable at different levels and in various ways [56].

The shells, with their changing, sometimes even playful character, full of surprises, with almost pyrotechnic, stupefying effects, are a dynamic, non-static object that does not tell us a single truth nor invite us to live a single, well-defined spatial experience, but wants to provoke our attention and curiosity through an emotional involvement; it wants to have the user participate in a complex, amazing experience, and so uses seductive weapons to attract him. Giant screens that transmit images, film, sliding text, bits of poetry or publicity slogans, stunning effects and plays of light, or great frescoes, optical illusions, are used as a means to impress the distracted passer-by, to promise him an exciting experience and not just to inform him of the building's role and the events that take place within it. It is a way to break with a tradition that has always provided a static, almost solemn, pompous setting, architectures that declared their institutional role already from the outside.

Renzo Piano described in this way his design intentions for the Centre Pompidou in Paris: "(...) I had always thought it was impossible to design a

Le Carceri, G. B. Piranesi, 1745-1750.

building according to the canons of the harmony of forms. Its function was so new, puzzling, full of unknowns, which made it a kind of spaceship, a UFO. I didn't know how but certainly had to forget the old canons, make a clean break with their pompous, solemn, intimidating mindset, and propose a solution that would attract people, overcome their distrust and awaken their curiosity".

Everything the shell-screens narrate and allow us imagine from the outside will find confirmation or perhaps also denial inside, in the nucleus where this world, hitherto unknown in its real potentialities, develops and reaches unimaginable results. It is a veritable microcosm, where actual reality and virtual reality so commingle as to make the continuous and different spatial experiences a "dosed amalgam between the conviviality of daily ritual and the strong emotions of exceptional events"[57].

Center Tods, T. Ito, Tokio, 2004.

Chapter 3

110

NOTES

1 Bordini 1994.
2 Secchi R. 1991.
3 Koolhaas, OMA, Mau 1995.
4 Secchi B. 1993.
5 "Their character of closed places allows besides a moderate overseeing that would be impossible in the open. There can be considered therefore by some persons as sure places and by others as buffer. The commercial activities that happen in the businesses and in the coffees they supply some possibilities of focused interactions, and the staff suited the sales is generally attentive to the good trend of the enterprise and it tries to avoid rising up of the problems. In other half-open places, actors and musicians are sometimes invited to perform in order that the passers-by feel themselves to own comfort and the social contacts are favored" (Rustin 1991, p. 55).
6 "In all that alternatives to the urban roads, they are appreciated above all for their certainty promise in a world that seems more and more threatening. (...) In the last years 'these places', thanks to their tried yield and the desirability like social catalysts, there have become an ideological choice for the organization of the contemporary urban life not only in the suburbs, but by now also in the heart of many cities" (Ingersoll 1992, p. 63).
7 Since Cenzatti and Crawford remember, the variations are great for example the atrium with skylight is, a prototype kind reproduced in the whole world. To find new manners of elaborating and of differentiating this space what, if no it remains generic and homogeneous, there have been born particular solutions that go to the creation of more and more extraordinary huge volumes, which nevertheless more times look like cathedrals with the "flooded naves of light what they remember more and more anonymous demonstrations of technical virtuosity" or the spaces creation consciously artificial that are brightened up "special effects which lifts that are immersed in fountains or they hole the roof, gardens hanging and you fall". The space of the foyer comes de - familiarized exaggerating the proportions it and through the use of a disorientated choreography of stratified spaces (Cenzatti, Crawford 1993, pp. 34-38).
8 See: Rowe, C., Koetter, F., 1979, *Collage City*, Cambridge, Mass., trad. it. 1981, Collage City, Milan, The Assayer; The analogous city of Aldo Rossi to La Biennale of Venice of 1976 "(...) Each work and each object - if the image of the own use does not want to get squashed above - possesses an own autonomy, it develops an own life - it seems, in any case, clear to me that the board returns in quite plastic way the image of the different meanings which different projects produce through an assembling comparatively arbitrarily; to take each mechanical value out or of mechanism to this construction the authors, more or less automatically, they have introduced things, objects, memories trying to express a dimension of the neighbourhood and of the memory" (Ferlenga 1989, pp. 118-119).
9 "The alteration completed by the Canaletto in the urban context of Venice speaks about the profound reality of such a city in XVIII century: of the fact, that is, that the most devastating manipulations are legitimate on a become urban organism, by now only a disposable object for the tourists' elite imagination. And it is sure that you are the Whims of the Canaletto, that the Sights, You Imprison them or the Campo Marzio they are, in their own way, 'it invites to the journey', advertising materials: the economic value of his incisions é quite present, as we know, to Piranesi, that it adopts a perspicacious strategy in order that his public attracts. Be Canaletto that Piranesi wants nevertheless the journey not to limit itself to a hedonistic sensations accumulating. In the journey it is necessary to be conscious that the desired adventure, to be a total, must have no limits, that then the journey is prolonged to the infinite, which at him it is not possible to make a return (...) by his nature the journey induces to a mental 'assembling': he can put peace again the traveler with the time and with the space, 'challenged' during the journey once 'returned to house'" (Tafuri 1980, pp. 55-56).
10 Benjamin 1955, pp.145-146.
11 "That this last is composed like a shapeless heap of fragments that butt one against other is immediately legible. The whole zone included between the Tiber, the Capitol, the Quirinale, the Pincio is set according to a method of arbitrary associations (even if Piranesi receives the suggestions of the Shape urbis), whose beginnings of aggregation exclude each organicity. (...) But it is clear, that the recognizability of such alignments is functional only to a greater highlight of the 'triumph of the fragment', which dominates the shapeless one there overlap illegitimate organisms of the Martian Field. Not at random, this assumes the faces of a homogeneous magnetic field, blocked by objects between extraneous them. Only with a remarkable effort it is possible to extract, that field, definite typological structures. And also established a complex casuistry of organisms based on triadic, polycentric laws, mixed lines or on virtuoso traced out drawing curves, this that is obtained is a kind of typological denial, of 'architectural banquet

of the nausea', of semantic gap for excess of visual noise" (Tafuri 1980, pp. 47-48).
12 Purini 1992.
13 Bordini 1994.
14 Thermes 1995.
15 Jameson 1984.
16 Thermes 1995.
17 Bonomi 1996.
18 Urry 1995.
19 Jameson 1984.
20 Bettetini 1995.
21 Ricoeur 1995.
22 Calvino 1993.
23 "If then the place is the original qualification of the space lived (and always built), he is also the system of the places, the place is not only the shelter in whom to be established, as he was saying Aristotele (the internal surface of the covering), but also the interval to be covered. (...) The placing of the action during the things is equivalent to mark the space with facts that intervene in the spatial disposition of the things, the story does not limit itself to a memories exchange, but it extends to runs that go of place to place. Be this space of allocation or circulation space, the built space consists in a rites system for the great changes of the life. The places are points in whom there happens something, in whom temporal changes follow real ways long intervals that separate and bring the places near" (Ricoeur 1995, pp. 64-66).
24 Bettetini 1995.
25 Koolhaas 2004.
26 Calvino 1993.
27 De Rossi 1996.
28 Mc Kean 1994.
29 Of the 1st Times May 1851, inauguration of Crystal Palace. (Petrilli, 1995, p. 126).
30 Of the 1st Times May 1851, inauguration of Crystal Palace in Petrilli, 1995.
31 To the point a Galerie des Machines, thirty eight slower years so the contemporary ones express themselves: "(...) in spite of the development of the beautiful lateral galleries, the look has difficulty to get used to these dimensions up to here unheard-of, and remains disconcerted to the presence of so many immensity. Also the depressed lancet arch of the arches deceives the eye and not to all the exact knowledge of the height of the building: the eye will get used a little to somewhat to these gigantic perspectives: on the first ones caught, it will finish admiring all of it. It is the vision of the big one" (De Parville, 1890, p. 62).
32 Nicolin 1996.
33 "The lift, with his possibility of creating mechanical connections architectural, and the complex of inventions that from him derive cancel and deprive the classic catalogue of the architecture (...)" (Koolhaas 1994, pp. 87-88).
34 Alberti 1450.
35 He does not love to himself, stressing the single parts of the whole, to consider fundamental again the experience of Durand, which was supporting fundamentally the predominant list of the elements in the possibility of composing them in a whole. To the contrary one it holds itself up what the power and the autonomy of the single parts, become autonomous and characterized entities, can check better and define a whole. Nevertheless without forgetting that the infinite variations can interpret that articulation, that complexity of activity, functions and meanings as which these new collective complexes require (Ugo 1991, pp. 127-131).
36 See: F. Purini, *L'architettura didattica*, Casa del libro editrice, Reggio Calabria 1980, pp. 56-58; P. O. Rossi, *La grammatica della fantasia*, in *La costruzione del progetto architettonico*, Laterza, Bari 1995.
37 Prestinenza Puglisi 1996.
38 "Exists a multiplicity of times, marked by irregular watches fixed to not rigid, arbitrarily chosen bodies of reference. Einstein calls these 'bodies', which are deformed during their motion through the action of the gravitational field, mollusks. The metropolis (but we might call it still so?) of the general relativity it is constituted at interacting of the movements of 'bodies' as mollusks indefinitely elastic. (Exercise: we imagine a continuous temporal-space in whom it always marks own had mollusks, and not times scanned on-equally of the pure succession, they vary in their shape according to the gravitational field in whom they are, in whom happened - and we imagine, even more, a whole that can be built from one any of such mollusks, a whole, that is, that may be built completely independently at the choice of the mollusk)" (Cacciari 1986, pp. 14-15).
39 "The external configuration is Usually rather simple, but inside an organism there is contained a surprising complexity of structures that have been for a long time the delight of the scholars. The specific shape of a plant or of an animal is determined not only by the genii and by the cytoplasmatic activity that these run, but also the interaction between genetic constitution and environment. A datum gene does not check a specific character, but a specific reaction to a specific environment" (Sinnott 1963, respondent in Venturi 1966, p. 86).
40 "Yo Plan at the external line the interior, produces a necessary tension that they help to make an architecture. If the outside produces a necessary tension that they help to make an architecture. If the outside differs on the inside, I point the wall of transition, it becomes an architectural fact: the architecture is when there are met internal and external forces of use and space. Such forces, internal and environmental, they are general and particular, principal and secondary. The architecture

Chapter 3

you look between interior and outside, it becomes the spatial record of this resolution and of his drama. And recognizing the difference between interior and outside, the architecture opens still once the doors to a way of thinking more tied to urban beginnings" (Next 1966, page 103).
41 Giambattista Nolli, New Plant of Rome of 1748.
42 "The application inside the type of spatial organization and of those materials that recall the external world returns the least cozy interior; to the same way the spatial reference to the internal world returns the coziest outside. Therefore to make interior and outside relative and together the ambiguity that I try this raises, intensifies in a space, be the sense of accessibility that that of intimacy. A sequence of indications obtained with architectural means ensures a gradual entry and an exit. The complex interior of experiences stimulated by this architectural means contributes to this process: gradations of height and width, of the level of illumination (natural and artificial), materials or different shares of trampling. Based on the recognition of preceding and similar experiences, different sensations within this sequence, evoke an associations variedness, each one of which corresponds to a different degree of 'inwardness' and 'externals'. Each sensation does not refer only to a specific degree of 'inwardness' and 'externals', but for extension it refers also to the corresponding use" (Hertzberger 1995, p. 80).
43 "To the age of his creation was the centre of the commerce of luxury and of the fashion, it was offering to the bourgeois public a theatre to be shown, to be presented, and the possibility of being amazed, improving, showing and consuming products of an industry of luxury in heat 'essor'. (...)

The passages were to the service of this public what one was feeling more to his comfort under the artificial light of the foyers of theatres, terraces of the coffees, of the great restaurants and bars, under the glass doors of the passages, in this atmosphere illusionist, this jungle built for the man, this reality under glass that substitutes the nature" (Benjamin 1982).
44 Rella 1982.
45 Geist 1969.
46 Hertzberger was describing so the knowledge of polyvalent space: "(...) since it is impossible (and it has always been it) to realize the individual environment that adapts exactly to each one, we must create the possibility of a personal interpretation, doing the things so that they are really interpretable" (Frampton 1980, p. 346).
47 It is the case of Guggenheim Museum to New York of Frank Lloyd Wright.
48 Dunlop 1996.
49 Harvey 1990.
50 Rella 1984.
51 Calvino 2012.
52 Cervellini 1996.
53 Foucault 1985.
54 Van Eyck 1962.
55 Zardini 1994.
56 Colafranceschi 1997.
57 From the project report for the pompidou center of R. Piano and R. Rogers.

4 Living place Living spaces: New hypotheses taking shape

> **"** With the demolition of the Berlin Wall five international architects were asked how the area adjacent to it could be revitalized. My suggestion was to turn on the light, because light is exactly like life and it was precisely what was missing in the area: light. (...) In Berlin buildings are usually grave and dull, and I on the contrary proposed a building whose inner life could be seen. (...) a building needs of life, people behind see-through glass walls; it needs the screen to be filled with different images. **"**

(J. Nouvel)

Galleria BCE, S. Calatrava, Toronto, 1994.

Transformation of what exists

One of the features of the contemporary city is that it is built mainly upon itself, and so we are continually faced with the problem of having to re-interpret, modifying places that are no more, in order to transform them into something that today we might call not yet. The opportunity lies in the availability of large complexes of the past that are waiting to be completely re-interpreted and serve new uses, and, once an overhaul of re-signification is carried out, to be given a new identity. They are places waiting to become hubs of attraction, emitting energy to the entire city.

There are several ways of reinterpreting existing buildings, some taking the more radical route of complete renovation, a total rethinking of the complex even in terms of language, while others involve more limited operations, maintenance of the original structure but completely changing their sense, re-signifying places by giving them a new roof or wrapping them in a new shell.

These operations preserve existing buildings from the decay to which they are subject, and, with the addition of new components, prepare and reinvent new uses and the expression of new languages, making it possible for a multiplicity of meanings to coexist, find new energy, new life and, above all, a new role within the city.

How an old building in a historic center, located in one of its most important and ancient streets, can be reborn and take on a strategic role within the city, has been the successful goal of a recent project in the center of Porto, in Portugal.

The complex, substituting an old building along the rua Catarina, whose façade alone was preserved to ensure the continuity of the street contour was developed within in a completely autonomous way, to make it a new relational hub, a great gathering place for the entire city.

The Rua Catarina Shopping Center is located inside a block set between two important city streets, and connects them by compensating for their height difference with its three levels, which relate to each other by way of a large courtyard covered by a light, transparent vault. It is a very large, open center in which a glass skylight, set back from the old façade, admits a glimpse of the new space, and then gradually exposes it at the point where, amidst a play of escalators, ramps and elevators, the visitor is drawn up to the third level, assigned mainly to the various refreshment spots.

When the visitor reaches this space, which functions as a real city square, it has become completely open and illuminated, giving him the distinct impression of being outside in one of the many areas of the historic center.

Rua Catarina Shopping Mall, Oporto.

This aspect is emphasized by the staging of a true urban situation through the reconstruction of a series of typical Portuguese street fronts, which go hand in hand with their characteristic elements of the main street, thus provoking a strong sensation of bewilderment, as occurs when an internal space seems like an external one, and the visitor finds himself in a public space which is actually a private one, and in an outside which is actually an inside. The sense of estrangement is enhanced by a strong glare that is dimmed somewhat by the printed glass whose lights and shadows reproduce the sensation of walking beneath the shade of sporadic awnings, typical of the streets of Spanish cities or certain Arab towns.

This level is the highest, surely the most significant; for once the visitor reaches it he is in direct contact with the other façade that overlooks a higher part of the city. A large screen has been placed here, projecting images, videos, runway shows, songs and concerts that accompany him on his roaming, serving as a nexus of participation and movement, thus enriching the spatial experience with new stimuli, allowing him to participate in the several events that take place there.

We have an acute sensation of walking through the center. We find ourselves in a new space, almost a new square that has sprung up amid the fabric of the past, preserving unaltered some of its original elements, such as the front façade on the Rua Catarina. The façade becomes a kind of mask in a game of cross-references between old and new, between the ordinary and the exceptional. So if on the one hand we seem to enter a historic building, one of many that make up the rua's street curtain, on the other we are catapulted into an extraordinary situation where, behind an ordinary façade, there lies an extraordinary event, a whole new world to experience.

The Rua Catarina Shopping Center features a new spatiality, almost a several-storied city. The lack of new areas for new projects within the ancient fabric has meant that the horizontal complexity that has always characterized the historic city is transformed here into a superimposed vertical complexity where we come and go in an up-and-down movement, in the same way we would cover the length and breadth of streets and squares.

The Center reinterprets and reproduces the spatial conformation that is typical of Porto (whose spatiality is characterized by steep slopes and constant altitude jumps) and concentrates it in a single area. But it misses the chance to reproduce that world full of overlapping spaces which is the city's hallmark. Bridges, elevators, walkways are the airy elements that in passing over the city determine the continued loss of orientation which provokes persistent confusion between an above and a below.

The traditional block has been loosely interpreted in Nouvel's design for a Multifunctional Center on Friedrichstrasse in Berlin. The intention is clear and specific: to transform the traditional elements of the Berlin block into something else that is exciting and fascinating, and it converts it from a serial, repeated element into an exception that makes it a hub of urban attraction, a new public place. This can only come about, as Nouvel himself suggests, by turning on the light, "because light is exactly like life, and this is precisely what is lacking in the area".[1]

Some basic choices make the block lighter than traditional ones. On the one hand, the recess of the top floors, on the other emphasis through a wide band of light, reminiscent of the crown and interval of string courses, which turns into a series of bands of frosted glass that envelop the volume, a clear reference to Erich Mendelsohn's Schocken Department Store in Stuttgart, exploiting it to scroll advertising captions, so that the space is already predisposed for commercial and publicity information, with no risk of future disfigurement of the building's appearance.

Within it is the idea of transforming the traditional patios, or rather the so-called classic cavaedia blocks, into true cones of light covered with various-sized mirrors that pierce the building and, besides admitting natural light at

Chapter 4

different levels, create a series of phantasmagorical effects through the use of rays of artificial and natural light, colors, flashes and movements. The cones of light almost dematerialize, helping to make this particular block an urban hub of attraction, a place capable of creating events.

The whole block is gathered around a larger inner cavity, a kind of square that connects the entire building from top to bottom through the mirror-covered light cones. The two big cones, starting from the ground floor, enter into contact, one with the sky and the other with the basement parking areas.

Galeries Lafayette, J. Nouvel, Berlin, 1996.

The mirrors that line the two large cones, through their concavity, produce a variety of effects, several reflections that offer glimpses of people at the various levels, and so we are in total communication with the whole building, as has always been the case with original department store structures, though here the immediate communication with the street allows us to perceive its inner life thanks to the beams of natural light. It is interesting to note that these inner hollows have been considered actual courtyards, so that the surface covering them has been treated as if it were a public surface that circulates messages.

One way to rethink some of these spaces in the contemporary city can start with the placement of a new roof. This type of intervention, while maintaining the original structure intact, allows a thorough revisitation, so that a variety of elements and activities can be concentrated within a complex yet single spatial structure, a kind of bell jar that succeeds in creating a city within a city[2].

It is a project that permits protection of all the pedestrian spaces from the weather, the creation of a safer, more comfortable environment through the control of bioclimatic factors. Above all, it permits a thorough rethinking of the variety of planned uses and functions, the integration of new languages and new, diverse meanings. The result is immediate: transforming a misconceived space into a great suburban square, a new meeting place for the community, like Nordwestzentrum in the suburbs of Frankfurt.

The metamorphosis takes place through an interplay of various factors: the inclusion of more naturalistic forms, such its lamellar structure, which softens the severity of the original buildings; the inclusion of natural elements in this space, making it more enjoyable and comfortable; the more direct link via escalators to the metro station, buses, taxis, with sub-level parking, and, lastly, the combination and revitalization of several activities, some of which purely commercial, others leisure[3]. The Paris fashion center of Jakob+Macfarlane took shape around existing reinforced concrete structures which were part of the Seine Docks system. It is configured as an interesting layered system, a new steel and glass skin that grew over the original reinforced concrete skeleton.

The new structure was born from the systematic deformation of the pre-existing construction module. As an example of the tree structure concept, the new building "springs" from the old one like a branch from a tree and offers visitors unexpected scenic views. The new shell, consisting of a lightweight steel and glass structure called a "plug-over", is designed to protect the existing building and its new features.

Chapter 4

Caixa Forum, Herzog e de Meuron, Madrid, 2008.

The complex of the Caixa Forum in Madrid, designed by the Swiss architects Herzog & de Meuron offers an interesting system of reuse of former Central Electricity. The building is ideally raised in order to create a system of exchange connection to the portion of the city. The brick building was completely gutted, demolishing the interior and the roof and leaving only a shell behind. Then they cut away the granite base to create the illusion that the building is hovering over the entrance plaza. The separation of the structure from the ground level created two worlds; one below and the other above the ground. The «underworld» buried beneath the topographically landscaped plaza provides space for a theater/auditorium, service rooms, and several parking spaces. The multi-storied building above ground houses the entrance lobby and galleries, a restaurant and administrative offices. There is a contrast between the flexible and loft-like character of the exhibition spaces and the spatial complexity of the top floor with its restaurant/bar and the offices. This creates an interesting play of difference undeniably reveals that the new life of the building and its new function as a center of quality and urban magnet for the city.

The idea is to create a sort of external wrap that protects the existing concrete structure and is able to constitute, at the same time, a new space in which to place pedestrian walkways and other functions. The project, besides hosting a variety of functions related to the theme of fashion and design in particular, exhibition spaces, the French Institute of Fashion, shops, a library, and dining and entertainment spots, extends the public walks overlooking the Seine and links up with neighboring districts, until it reaches the panoramic roof, where it falls into a kind of feedback loop which allows the building to nestle integrally into its urban surroundings.

Lining completely with a new shell, an authentic garment: the idea is to revive old and obsolete building complexes without interfering in any way with their original structure, thus offering them a range of otherwise unattainable options for renewal.

This is the case with the Fresnoy Center in Tourcoing, an old complex from the twenties, completely relined by a new hyper-technological shell that enables new functions to be included, the creation of new spaces and new technical and expressive opportunities. The construction of a new in-between space between the large shell and the pre-existing elements below needs to be verified, and this is what happens in the idea of a complete relining with a new shell, a real makeover for old, disused, obsolete complexes, without disturbing the original structure.

The space generated by the placement of a box which contains a number of other boxes is a new space created by the revitalization of old buildings and will be reshaped into a space for the 21st century. A big box that contains other boxes. This new ultra-technological shell, which makes possible the protection of the existing volumes from the weather and the redevelopment of the complex in the terms of a new language, is formed by a large metal-structured roof which, in addition to letting through all the ventilation, heating and air-conditioning machinery, is lighter and more luminous by virtue of its great, irregular-shaped, cloud-like openings; by a completely closed curtain wall façade; and by two completely open sides that allow the whole to be completely transparent.

We can speak here more of an architecture-event than of an architecture-object. Even the space itself, in the interplay between its new and old roofs, becomes a place of fantasies and experiments within a new space conceived with new standards and ideas. Through this fusion a space is created that Tschumi defines as "unprecedented". This space, not intended at first to be lived in and seemingly a residue between the big box and the various inner boxes, becomes a world to be discovered and explored by way of a series of ramps, walkways and stairs[4].

City of Fashion and Design, Jakob + MacFarlane, Paris, 2008.

Cover hypothesis for the space in front of Pompidou Centre, Y. Friedman.

Wrapped trees, Christo, 1988-98.

Chapter 4

These spaces can host events, performances, cinemas, restaurants and bars, all of it stimulated by the unusual and fascinating rooftop world of the original structures. Even the intrados of the new roof becomes an opportunity for spectacle, predisposed as it is not only for the installation of machinery but also for "passing" information and advertising.

The elements that make up the project are several and can be combined among them in various ways, since everything takes place under the big roof, as a common denominator or great umbrella summarizing all these differences; the materials themselves are varied and gathered together by the shell. The large roof's intrados and the northern façade are made of steel, while the eastern and southern façades are glass curtain walls; lastly, the pre-existing elements stand out in the duly restored masonry.

Reintroducing archetypes

At the origin of these considerations is the reintroduction of archetypes as a primitive principle which enables us to start from scratch in defining these new places and discovering how this can be done principally with one of the building's basic elements, and stressing the transposition of a part such as the roof or the basement with respect to the whole through the rhetorical device of synecdoche.

The identification of certain categories of intervention, certain modes of collocation within a city, is one possible way of beginning to interpret these places and their configuration and to understand how, through many complex variables, we can explore a path that seems to tie together some of the most important examples of these new public places in a quest for original forms, toward elementary forms and their archetypal substance.

The elementary forms that different modalities of architectural space take on constitute in their archetypal substance genetic principles whose structure coincides with their place. They are representations of their own virtuality and their theoretical capacity as developed within the language where all their strength and truth reside[5].

These places, in substance, re-propose archetypal forms as basic forms to start from in order to establish a new way of placing key points in the city. The original, basic forms are: the cabin as possible shelter; the basement as an underground, often labyrinthine space; the bridge as a suspended, versatile element. The opportunity of considering such forms as foundational enables us to start from scratch in order to stress possible future meanings. Since we

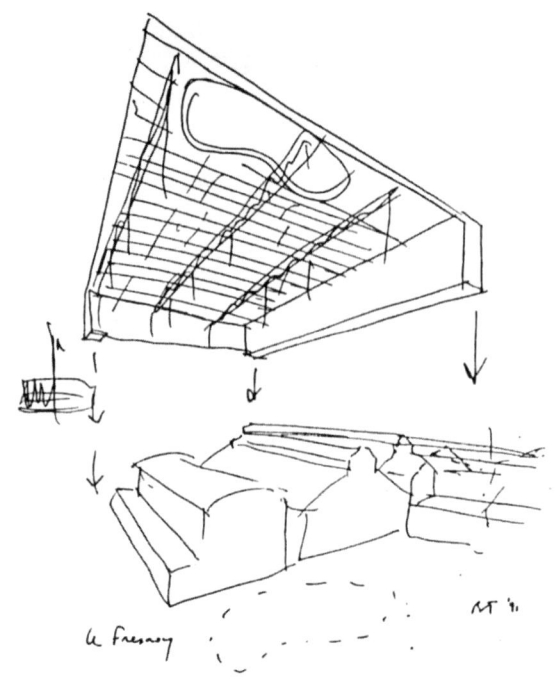

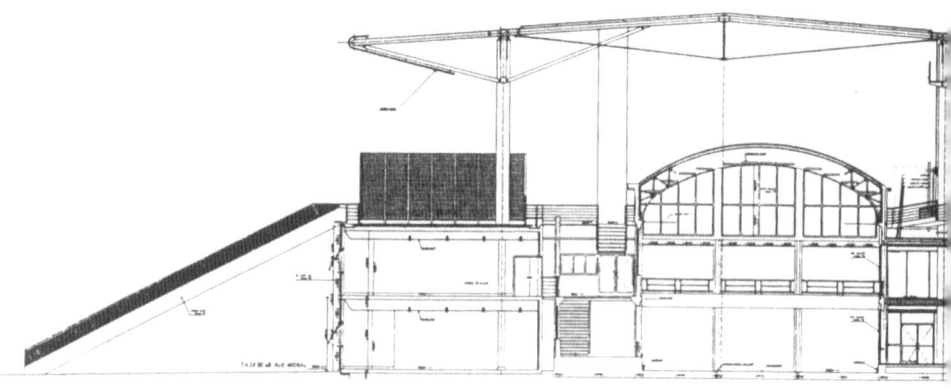

The National Studio for Contemporary Arts, Le Fresnoy, Tourcoing, B. Tschumi Architects, 1997. (drawing, axonometric projection and cross section)

Chapter 4

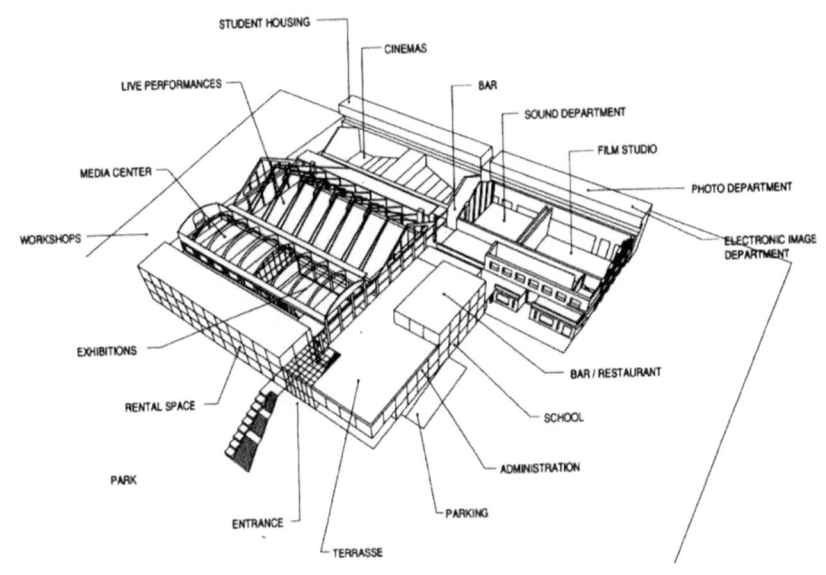

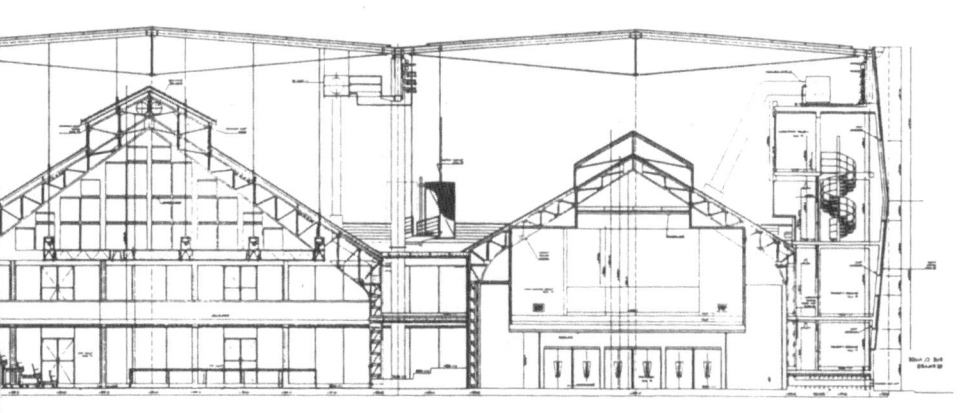

are dealing with a complexity containing infinite variables, starting from the original architectural concepts allows us, in regard to these new places, to establish an initial identification and then to apply stratification of additional meanings and relationships; at the basis, however, there is the opportunity to express a clear, recognizable concept.

Actually, this classification made according to a correspondence to archetypal models is a bit forced, since in architecture there is always an imperfect coincidence that is concretized in a broad spectrum of maneuver, a play of possibilities among the various combinations that is simultaneously the enigmatic trap of a labyrinthine path, the system of rules that organizes the materials of nature in the clarity of the cabin, and the element suspended between heaven and earth, a place of transit and commerce.

Nevertheless, it was found that, in proposing a classification of this type, there exist constants of placement due on one hand to the objective presence of particular conditions that must be dealt with by inserting these multifunctional hubs within extremely well-established structures, and on the other to the presence of certain recurrent features of extreme heterogeneity, which suggests that we can proceed with the application of a great unifying element: a single great roof.

Being able to use both the underground and above-ground portions is certainly an interesting answer to the lack of space in order to be able to fit these new places of social relations within the traditional structure of the city.

The creation of an overlap of levels that can constantly interact makes it possible to provide a part of the cultural and social services that are currently lacking in the urban context. And since they are complex, articulated spaces and places, which must be continuously and intensely perceived and experienced, they can be configured as underground elements by using the city's subterranean heritage, thus becoming basement-buildings, large multifunctional complexes of spaces and services that, by their rootedness in the depths of the earth, totally identify with their attachment to it and with the archetype of the labyrinth.

Finally, elements that loom over the city in great airy complexes, by using an available space that is almost infinite, can become immensely interesting solutions that redevelop parts of the city lacking in public spaces.

The cabin, the labyrinth and the bridge, as archetypes and theoretical models, are Ur-forms representing an extreme aspect, liminal conditions in which, as Vittorio Ugo says, "the architectural substance and the theoretical structure of building are condensed to a maximum"[6].

The great roof

Where a roof is used as a unifying element, this tends to become the matrix and identification of the whole project.

The site offers an inclusive aura that incorporates within it all possibilities, making them practicable under a great roof that permits all and protects all.

The cabin archetype has always been a refuge, a shelter; Alberti already identified it as a system of static perfection based on the notions of concinnitas and mediocritas, as parts of the body that "fully correspond to each other, to the point of being able to calculate with ease the sizes of them all by measuring just one of them"[7]; for Filarete it is directly Adam and the shape of his body, when he takes refuge beneath his hands, which provide a representation of the archetype of the primitive cabin[8].

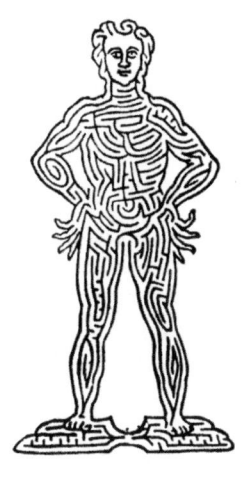

Adam forms a sheher for himself from the rain with his arms, Filarete, Treatise on architecture, 1460.

Labirinth as a man.

The cabin has always implied a sense of shelter, of certain stability and the possibility of dwelling, and has always been, since antiquity, the reference point from which we start and to which we return. The idea of the house, the cabin, the tent as a natural product of man, whose aim is to satisfy his needs and to neutralize the drawbacks of the natural environment, is at the basis of the design of these places, which, through an operation of synthesis, we might call roof-buildings. In them there is an attempt to bring together in one great element all the complexity of the city, to achieve a sort of recomposition of fragmentedness through the creation of a world apart.

What predominates in these places is a desire for protection from the city itself, from bad weather and pollution, and to find shelter from the most varied forms of violence. This can be done in different ways through all the possible interpretations of the theme of shelter: from a wholly virtual roof, to a roof that becomes, through its acutely inclined shape, a kind of fifth façade, to a roof that is identified with an element of the landscape, such as hills, to a large tent in an open field. Lastly, one more variation on the theme of the cabin-shelter is to be found in a great roof in the form of a ship's hull which doubles as a haven lighthouse.

A wholly virtual roof is what Frank Gehry designed for Festival Disney at the Disney Park in Marne-la-Vallée in Paris, a multifunctional hub of about 18,000 square meters located at the park's exit. Here a grid of pillars encompasses a series of buildings that do not follow the line of the pillars but are placed in a deliberately irregular, disjointed manner, thus determining unusual irregularities, randomness and juxtapositions that provoke a severe tension, although the sense of instability is compensated at the top by an imaginary roof.

Simulation becomes here an architectural theme. The pillars are sheathed with aluminum plates bearing a geometric pattern that mimics the twisted columns, providing a sense of motion. The extremely light, almost non-existent roof is realized by a series of wires connected together like an abstract foundation grid in preparation for a hypothetical construction, almost a scaffold. By night it is transformed into a roof made up of laser-seeming light beams that intersect in the sky to form an immense hypothetical shell of protection. The shining, sparkling wires form a myriad of glowing dots that create a luminous shelter, a kind of starry sky above our heads.

What by day is a scarcely visible, virtual roof, at night turns into a great luminous sombrero, a covering full of light, which seems to dematerialize completely in contact with the intensity of the night sky. The roof is there, one feels it, although it is really just a frame serving as a theme for the continual confusion between reality and fantasy which lies at the core of Disney's world.

Gehry skillfully interprets the combination of reality/make-believe, provoking in his work a sense of bewilderment. The surprise effect is certainly exciting, as one perceives and experiences it in crossing this space, and it is pulled off without any need to resort to another language, borrowed from the world of Mickey Mouse, without having to rely on false historical settings, or worse, images drawn from futuristic visions.

Festival Disney fulfills its entertainment function in no uncertain way by reproposing an area of city streets and squares where people can eat and walk, and Gehry interprets it in a contemporary fashion, with a particular eye for the concept of mass tourism, which he wants to entertain, distract and lure away from everyday life. He does not draw on the fantasy world of cartoons, as this has become hackneyed through endless repetition and is no longer

Festival Disney, Disneyland, F. Gehry, Paris, 1992.

representative of the essential features of freshness, fantasy and imagination. It has all been seen, experienced and exported down to its minimal details, a world already imagined, without leaving any space for the unsaid, the invisible, the force of imagination.

In another context, in the new district of Euralille in the city of Lille, the new center designed and built by Jean Nouvel is, with its variety of commercial, residential, tertiary and cultural functions, one of the city's hubs of attraction, soon to become an important node of trade with the rest of Europe. The Center, which by no accident bears the name of the whole district, lies beneath a large sloping roof as a mediating element of the city's new overall role.

The idea was to create an event, and this place, precisely on account of its complexity, variety and articulation, was designed to become a vector of energy. It is an alternative part of the city which, precisely on account of the production of trade, culture, events and entertainment that can take place inside, becomes pivotal for redeveloping the surrounding area and especially for the future development of the city. The great roof with its acute inclination, which becomes almost a fifth façade, is composed of perforated metal elements that create special plays of light which differ over the course of the day, to create a veil between the interior and the exterior, which, through different depths and unusual lighting effects, is perceived as a great shifting sky. Like a real city under a large roof, the space, punctuated by large pillars covered with reflecting material, which seems to constantly dematerialize, offers multiple inner passageways, among which one, the most important, is a kind of diagonal that connects the city center to two different stations and forms a single great internal agora, a main meeting place and a multi-level point of access and trade. As Nouvel himself states, the design of the Euralille Center's roof was a project in its own right. Rem Koolhaas had planned it as a landscape in itself. It covers a nearly four-acre area, a fact that utterly ruled out a normal, traditional roof. From the large roof rise five towers placed at intervals along the main street to form an interesting urban signal with their long ground plane down Avenue Willy Brandt, hosting offices, schools and an apartment complex, the only elements that, to some extent, with their height and seriality, counterbalance the infinite extension of the roof.

For the new community center located in a narrow area between the hill and the outskirts of Saitama, Japan – i.e., the Saitama Arena – Renzo Piano designed a roofing profile that emulates the landscape's geographical undulation. The roof-shaped hill, in reproducing nature metaphorically, seeks to impose itself on the territory with the same prominence with which the hills in Japanese cities suddenly emerge from the gray urban fabric. It is as if the shell-like

Chapter 4

hill were generated by a slight telluric movement, "this time friendly", which compresses the space between the two railway lines to the east and west of the site and forces it into a gentle corrugation. It is a public space that has the quality and the force of a geographical event, which enters the city's topography in a clear, grandiose contrast to an ancient temple, which is another great magnetizing element located to the north. The ambition is to enrich the city with an instrument of which the city is still ignorant but which could guarantee, today, the same unifying role than in other historical moments places of culture and entertainment have always played, ensuring conviviality in the daily ritual, and the powerful emotions of exceptional events.

It is a powerful, recognizable magnet, a true microcosm in which reality and virtual reality get confused in a new generation public place never before seen for its scale and complexity, and for its capacity to accelerate commerce. Just as twenty years ago the Centre George Pompidou was the invention of a new model of approach to traditional culture, so Saitama will be the citadel of the metropolitan culture of the future.

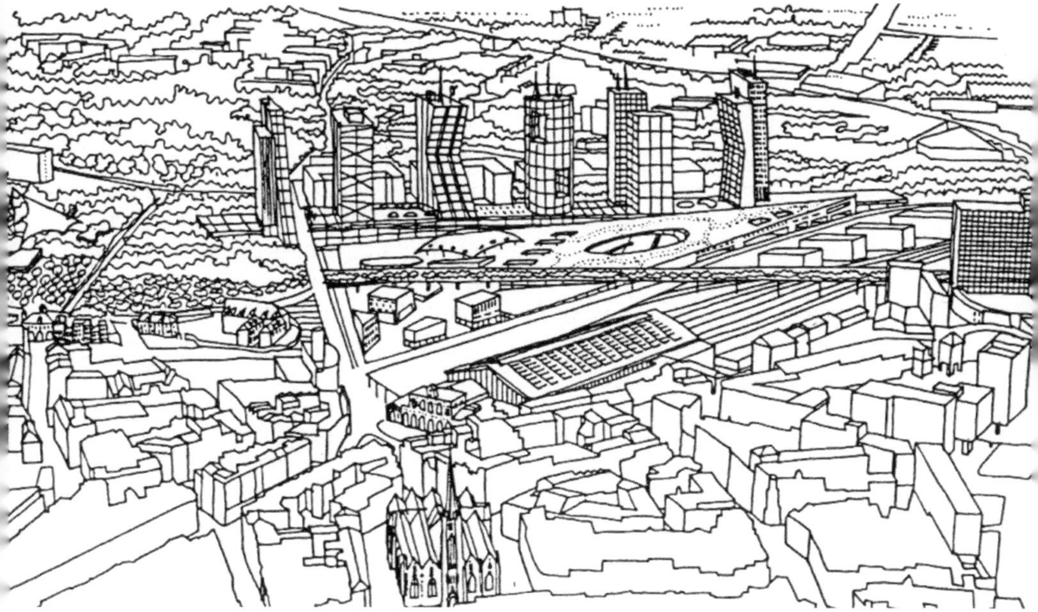

Masterplan Euralille, R. Koolhaas, Lille, 1994.

The center consists of a true citadel on several floors, a modern Tower of Babel, perhaps more orderly but just as lively, meant for cultural and commercial activities. Inside the large space shows a high degree of flexibility: it can be completely transformed by rising and lowering the floor and changing the visual and acoustic features with mobile screens set into the high ceiling. Saitama, in Piano's words, could play the role of a secular temple where the rites of our society are carried out, and at the same time, thanks to a play of spatial vibrations, lightness of details, the use of natural light, a pleasant natural setting and a multiplicity of possible functions, it could also be a new invention, a public space the size of a stadium, as changeable as a theater and as flexible as a modern instrument of communication.

The chance to study an interesting bioclimatic shell which covers a series of buildings, thus creating an in-between space between a pre-existence and a new roof, is offered by some experimental projects developed during the reconversion of Germany's Ruhr Valley. The area – particularly polluted because until the eighties of the 20th century it was martyred by intense mining activities that had produced an uncontrolled accumulation of slag from industrial processes and huge chasms from strip-mining – had posed a difficult problem of territorial and economic reconversion. In this context the French Jourda and Perradin group developed its project for the construction of a training center in the area of Herne-Sodingen, envisioning a large, neutral, theoretically extensible container. The idea was to create a new urban center which would be an engine for the future development of the city and the entire region, through the creation of a complex incorporating public and commercial facilities, and housing facilities of varying sizes; a great protective box of glass and wood, within which the buildings would be arranged almost to recreate a small urban microcosm, to host government offices, libraries, restaurants, small temporary dwellings and a green system, an authentic garden lush with Mediterranean vegetation.

The goal was to transform a heavily contaminated, polluted site into a socially and environmentally high-profile center. The glass enclosure creates a large, semi-public space endowed with the excellent, exceptionally pleasant living conditions of a mild climate and no rain. The main street is treated as a centralized urban space, and the inner volumes are designed with the principal aim of creating an environment on an urban scale, where the urban character of its internal space is generated by the interstitial spaces between the building volumes and the protective structure. The roof is made up of photovoltaic panels that are grouped to form a cloud-effect, creating shade and preventing excessive brightness.

Basement as metaphor of the labyrinth

Some places, as already mentioned, are transformed into complexes built entirely or partially underground, and realizing, through an operation reminiscent of synecdoche, a transposition of a part for the whole. These basement-buildings are in fact characterized by an attempt to identify with their attachment to the earth, becoming a kind of excavation architecture, housed in an underground world, and, through the configuration of underground structures, fitting into a network of service facilities and a series of new spaces that would otherwise be unthinkable within the well-established city.

Exploiting underground space makes possible the achievement of two interesting results: on the one hand, it responds to a lack of facilities in that part of the city, and on the other it creates an especially attractive point for the whole city.

The city's public space, which offers a new, possible way of living, is created by a stratification of levels, whose subterranean layer furnishes the well-established city with a powerful magnet capable of recreating an authentic microcosm. True reality and virtual reality merge together to become a new-generation, as yet unhabitual, never before seen public place in its complexity and ability to accelerate the chances for encounter commerce and leisure in the very heart of the city.

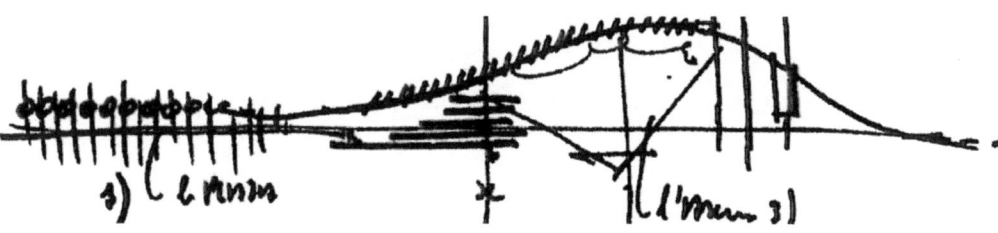

Saitama Arena, R. Piano, Saitama, Japan, 1995.

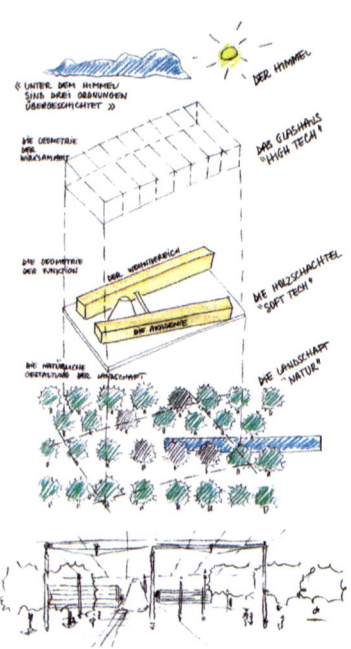

Herne-Sodingen Academy, Jourda and Perraudin, Ruhr valley, 1998. (sketches and view)

The building of such sites can redevelop and redesign parts of the city and, in contrast with the past, when the exploitation of underground spaces was mainly dictated by concerns for protection from adverse weather and defense from enemies, today this possible utilization represents an altogether new opportunity, especially for densely urbanized areas, a new possibility for placing within the established city a series of services it lacks. It is an almost unexplored resource that can also contribute greatly to redefining the image of the city and that can go a long way toward appropriating a renewed identity.

The inclusion in the city of subterranean public spaces, beyond representing with their coagulating and inspirational force a magnet for the entire surroundings, as is the case with all centers, also functions as a system of places that, in its special relationship "with the very bowels of the earth, and with an excavation toward the chthonic depths", reinterprets the labyrinth archetype, which is seen as an original element, a principle that in itself can epitomize a set of primeval values for architecture[9].

Recourse to the labyrinth archetype triggers a kind of purification, a catharsis, as if it were necessary to start from the reinterpretation of archetypal forms to be able to think of a complexity of situations, spaces, and modes of conditions to be contained in these places.

The labyrinth as structure and as idea, while on the one hand it is characterized as a place of security, isolation from the outside world and as a capacity to build a world unto itself, on the other it is characterized by the pleasure it provides of losing ourselves and possibly rediscovering ourselves, of knowing and recognizing, through the complete loss of orientation and bewilderment in having finally found the solution: the way out. Every point of reference with the outside is futile; a portion of space and time is isolated, absolutely other, qualitatively different from everyday experience, topography, geography or ordinary geometry. Thus there is established a universe conclusive in itself, without any external space and time, where it is difficult or almost impossible to cast a comprehensive glance that constructs a unified image and where it is not necessary to have a simultaneous, synthetic knowledge. In these places the emotional experience of play is generated by a special mood of surprise, distress, coming from the loss of control, from the loss of center, from losing oneself in a space with no beginning or end, and where one experiences the constant, simultaneous presence of real reality and virtual reality. Given the loss of external reference points, these places are often planned as Daedalic structures, associated as they are with a set of opposites that makes them especially attractive: from cunning to compulsion,

De Citadel complex,
C. de Portzamparc,
Almere (Holland), 2006

Designed by OMA group, perfectly placed in the project for the new city center in the newtown of Almere, Holland, the block designed by C. de Pontzamparc is interesting for its idea of vertical citadel where the layers overlap many functions. The idea is a large green cover, an "artificial hill", that hovering above the ground, contains within it a number of activities and uses, and it is transformed into a roof-park viable. Crossed by two roads, Despite being a new concept, it fits perfectly in the context, giving the impression of an organic growth with the historical city, the citadel as well as it has been called by Pontzamparc, recreates the density of a medieval town and it is paradigmatic his program a variety of uses, from bottom to top it houses the car park, the underground infrastructure, service shops, residences until the green cover inhabited.

from complexity to desire, and from rationality to the eagerness of quest and adventure[10].

The labyrinth as a product of the game of artifice is in a certain sense also the product of research and choice. On the one hand it identifies itself as a place of challenge, as the problematic game that, in order to be solved requires knowledge and/or artifice, and surely intelligence and cunning; on the other there is a game of references, combinations, continual bifurcations whose numerous ramifications must be chosen.

It is a place of flux, continual crossing, travel and recurrent discovery of novelty, and is aptly identified with a coming-and-going motion and with the ceaseless stream of people that, in utilizing the nodes of commerce, travel, tread, cross.

The subterranean placement of these centers also boasts another advantage: it poses no issues of language; it is not an element that creates difficult questions to resolve on contact with pre-existences. The absence of façades, the non-existence of a shell, and the consequent lack of a representative function make it conducive to freer interventions.

Labyrinth graffiti on a red pillar in the house of Lucrezio in Pompei.

The light-capturing elements become outer signals, precise references, which on the one hand have the important function of introducing light to the inside of the complex and on the other of indicating the presence of this system of spaces and identifying its rendezvous points, those special places for relaxation within the more complex system.

These basement-buildings can be set both within the actual historical centers or at any rate in well-established areas, with street-level constructions, and where it is desired to maintain at street-level a prevalently green area, as in the case of Les Halles, where the demolition of the 19th-century market freed up a large portion of urban space in the center of Paris. The idea in itself of demolishing the old market was certainly debatable, yet it made possible the construction of a new, large, multi-purpose complex, thus making up for the scarcity of new public meeting places in the city center.

The great influx of people is made possible in this place, beyond its strategic position for the development of a great commercial center, in its underground sector, where several subway lines, the regional railway and parking areas coincide. Thus a nodal point is formed, from which to begin the entire project.

A center of cultural and recreational services at the neighborhood and city level, a great commercial hub, a variety of play and sports activities, a concentration of vegetation, and more, represent the potential of the entire complex. Having been conceived as an underground place precisely in order to furnish the historic city center with a wide range of services without imposing added volume, it reduces the problem of language, and not least frees up part of the surface space overhead.

Underground areas confirm themselves, especially in large city centers, as a potential resource for the creation of social and cultural hubs, otherwise impossible to place, and an interesting contribution for the development and redevelopment of parts of the city by providing new uses, new functions, new ways of relating and meeting. A further possibility of establishing these multi-functional hubs is offered by the need to expand and enrich certain structures whose organization and function have become obsolete. This is the case, for example, of the Louvre Museum, for which, once the space was vacated after the definitive transfer of the Finance Ministry to Bercy, the opportunity was taken to completely rethink the museum's organization, structure and especially its role. For its comprehensive reorganization the architects Pei and Macary studied the possibility of intervening with an underground project which, in addition to providing a possible extension, would enrich the museum complex itself and the entire city of Paris with a series of appurtenances,

Social and cultural centre CaixaForum, A. Isozaki, Barcelona, 2002.

The Caixa Forum building in Barcelona, designed by Arata Isozaki, is interesting for its new basement with its series of new activities beneath the original Fabrica. The contrast is incisive: above an old modernist factory building designed by Puig i Cadafalch and built in brick to look almost like a medieval castle; and below a new architecture in white stonework that adds new activities to the historic factory, giving it new life.
At the entrance, to mark the change of use, a large tree-shaped canopy and a great excavation around the building brashly signal the site's enlargement and the newness of its functions. The connection between the two can be seen both inside and out, through a system of ramps and stairs reaching from street level to basement level. The enlargement, manifested by this semi-underground basement, offers a range of services, a large lobby, conference rooms, a library, a bookstore, and dining spaces, all, even internally, strictly linked to the factory complex above. With the realization of this project the CaixaForum has become one of the most dynamic and active cultural and meeting centers in Barcelona, hosting exhibitions, concerts, conferences, events and a gamut of activities.

public spaces and meeting facilities. The main concern was to provide the Louvre, as with all the world's great museums, with a number of support services, so that the public could spend more time there, prolonging and interrupting their visits, to rest and to use the refreshment spots comfortably and pleasantly. The idea was to design an underground strip of the city by exploiting the need to capture light to create great urban squares, meeting places, where powerful, significant, almost out-of-scale architectural elements serve to orient and join together[11]. The Carousel gallery, located below the square and garden level, aside from being a new entrance to the museum, introduces the visitor to spectacular public spaces which include department stores, concert halls of various seating capacities, and spaces of conviviality. It also provides an opportunity to visit the archaeological remains of the old fortress of Charles V, which came to light during the excavations, and ample parking for cars and public transport .

An especially effective proposal in this regard was to include a series of underground urban public spaces, otherwise impossible to join to the urban fabric of the historic city center, creating below street-level the fragment of another city. The Louvre's underground system has thus reproduced almost metaphorically an urban complexity which is often canceled in the contemporary city, and through a series of stratifications and events has transformed itself into a powerful, important element of the city's image, not only a place to host public activities but above all a cutting-edge instrument with its force as hub of aggregation and reorganization strategies for the city's central areas.

The City of Culture, designed by Peter Eisenman in the Spanish city of Santiago de Compostela, takes shape as a great ground system obtained from the superposition of a pair of two-dimensional traces, each of which cuts in a different way through the terrain: the trace of the old medieval town and the superimposition of an orthogonal Cartesian grid. These in turn are intersected by a third three-dimensional trace which follows the particular topography of the hill, distorting the two flat geometries to create an articulated system of recumbences. The terrain is curved, deformed, and the construction becomes one with it. This portion of the landscape houses all of the center's functions, which one discovers by proceeding along both the inner and outer spaces.

The project provides a system of indoor and outdoor places whose interstitial spaces, composed of different paths, ascents, descents, spaces of light and shaded areas, form a fragment of other cities whose atmosphere is distinctly Mediterranean. This furrowed land forms a place that is in perfect harmony with the landscape, from which it is born as a great multi-dimensional "crack" that allows it to be experienced in different ways.

Les Halles, P. Berger e J. Anziutti, Parigi, 2007-2016.

Following the demolition of the modular structures of steel and glass designed by Victor Baltard in 1854, the Les Halles complex has undergone various stages of transformation, the first Vasconi's Forum in 1976, followed by Chemetov's nearby Sant-Eustacle location in 1986, and lastly Berger and Anziutti's 2007 project, has been completed in 2016. Beyond certain questionable choices that imposed themselves after the demolition of the market, the area has become a marvelous public place that is a model for the large square of the future. The continuous movement guaranteed by the numerous means of transport constrains or attracts thousands of people, who, once swept into this mechanism, are fascinated by its endless possibilities.

The maritime terminal in Yokohama, designed by F.O.A. (Foreign Office Architects), is conceived as a large public space connected non-discontinuously to the mainland. It is a great inhabited land surface viable at multiple levels where the terminal itself, located at the middle level, is composed of a system of services and parking below, and the large public space above becomes a true urban plaza that can be used in many different ways: for concerts, sports festivals, cultural events and exhibitions, or just to wander around in and enjoy the landscape surrounded by water. The surface, bending several times on itself, forms folds that contain all the possible paths. The building is a true extension of the city, where an immense, undulating, inhabited terrain, an artificial landscape, becomes a place available to all. This interesting mix of functions has a special morphology whose many suggestions inspired it: the

Les Halles, Victor Baltard Paris, 1854 (archive image)

memory of a man-made beach of dunes, the long bridge of a ship or maybe just the shape of a huge whale skeleton that has barely breached the water surface. It is practicable in all different ways, a place devoted to fun, where the promenades of the citizens of Yokohama and those of passing boats mingle and intersect in a new landscape available to all.

Cars enter this complex machine made up of a never-ending series of lateral sections whose pattern includes endless variations. The lateral section of the terminal is formed by the multiple variations of this portal, while the increasingly elongated longitudinal section extends seawards, vying with the majesty of the great ships that dock there.

Eliminating mono-directionality in favor of multiple directions, all possible directions; this furrowed, inhabited ground, covered almost entirely by wooden surfaces, also has a static function: the weights are distributed along the inclined surfaces, thus concentrating the vertical forces on two points, to form a simple, functional three-hinged arch.

In the redevelopment project of the waterfront and ferry terminal in Santa Cruz de Tenerife in the Canary Islands, the architects Herzog and de Meuron adopted the interesting strategy of a kind of inhabited infrastructure. The theme was offered by the redevelopment of a waterfront where the creation of a public place equipped with businesses, services and a series of open spaces and walks overlooking the sea, connects the island with the sea and then with the whole world. The area, on the border between the port and the city itself, is transformed into a great strip dotted by businesses that wind along the entire perimeter to form an artificial terrain capable of servicing both the port and the city.

A new landscape is created, one that knits together land and sea, a new topography that, by incorporating through the invention of new public spaces parts of what already exists, reorganizes this border area between the city, the harbor and the sea. On the one hand, the city embraces the sea, and on the other the sea reappears in the city after having been relegated to the edge by the latest urban planning.

In Genoa, the Ponte Parodi area, centrally located within the new reorganization of the port, was chosen to become a center of international importance, serving the city culturally and recreationally. The Dutch architect Ben van Berkel, winner of the competition, proposed creating a new skyline facing the sea through the creation of a large public place, a great inhabited square on the sea edge.

Chapter 4

The square consists of an extensive inhabited terrain molded so as to be lived at different levels with different activities ranging from recreation, such as beaches and sports facilities, to accommodation, culture and commerce. The area below hosts shops, offices, studios, a cinema, a cruise terminal, an auditorium, and underground car parks, while in the overlying area a great livable roof by day and by night, overlooking the water and the harbor, becomes a vast privileged place of aggregation overlooking the city and the sea.

The City of Culture, P. Eisenman, Santiago de Compostela, 2011.

Carousel du Louvre, Grand Louvre, I. M. Pei e M. Macary, Paris, 1993.

The bridge-building

The construction of a bridge, even in temporally and geographically remote civilizations, has always carried with it a sense of sacrilege against nature, against the gods, against the order of the Cosmos. Bridges as an original principle have always been complex structures, organic intersections between nature and artifice, critical points of unstable forces, constructions between the flow of something that passes and the staticity of their structures; bridges as such are precise modes of existence of architectural space[12], which possess the dynamic nature of pathways, but also and above all the capacity to attract the attention of both the city and the entire territory[13].

Bridges are a syntactical element represented by a synthetic principle, an original archetype which can bring together, muster, rally, unify, and establish continuity. Georg Simmel, in Brücke und Tür (Bridge and Door), unites these two elements in his consideration that both represent a situation, a concept that favors communication and expresses the idea of conjunction and transition and "the will of connection which becomes the shape of things".

Like doors, bridges imply the topological dimension of continuity/discontinuity, relating to "the power to bind and loose which, in contrast to nature, is given by man, and in this specific way: that the one is always a prerequisite of the other"[14].

Bridges are meant to be places that gather the land as region around the river and constitute a polarity, so often assuming the role and character of center. This is characterized by its hinge function. Both bridges and doors articulate space, polarize and change it in a place with which they are ready simultaneously to assemble and therefore exchange.

Bridges, like cabins and labyrinths, represent a mode of existence of architectural space and can be analyzed and evaluated in their basic structure through the formulation of a diagram. Precisely because of this feature they are considered the result of a process of formation, material worked within the range defined by the theoretical forms identified in the three archetypes.

Bridges, as an original archetypal element capable of generating around itself a centrality, have always been an ambiguous, powerful element capable of generating spatial complexity, and possess an inherent predisposition to be considered a key element in the reorganization of certain urban areas. Bridges transformed into bridge-buildings become new public places which by virtue of their dual role are open to acquiring several meanings. The bridge-building,

International Sea Terminal, FOA Foreingn Office Architects, Yokohama, 1995-2002.

Chapter 4

as a place of collective urban complexity that makes it possible to reinvent the complexity which is an inherent urban element, to reconcile different values and practices that till the present moment have been devalued and distorted by their overly rationalistic isolation (through a strong cohesion of different functions, a semantic and spatial richness and a variety of commercial, cultural, leisure, and residential activities), and, precisely because of its spatial structure, to overcome the isolation of functions and citizens, and the separation of different urban components.

These complexes, which exploit a theoretically unlimited aerial plane, can provide interesting solutions to various difficult situations that cities continually face. The chance to create a public place that is cut off from the city level can solve functional problems of traffic, can overcome breaks that have formed in the urban fabric, can overcome height differences that constitute

"*Tenerife Espacio de las Artes*" (TEA) Herzog e de Meuron, Santa Cruz de Tenerife, Canary Islands, 1999-2008.

altitude leaps, and can be an element of great interest in reorganizing the problem areas of cities, even the most peripheral ones, that are in need of public facilities and services.

Public places configured as bridge-buildings are one of the possibilities for including discrete spatial elements in a more or less established urban context and, by metaphorically offering a complexity, reinvent an element of urban complexity by now canceled from the contemporary city, creating above it a fragment of a different city.

This type of intervention imitates in some sense a mechanism of urban growth made of an overlapping of meanings, an idea of construction that has never been interrupted in its dynamics. In the end, the building-bridge "seems to signify an overlapping, a juxtaposing of stratified signs in history or in the metaphorical values that accompany the very bridge idea", and thus harshly

Parodi Bridge, Ben van Berkel - UNStudio, Genova, 2001–2014.

153

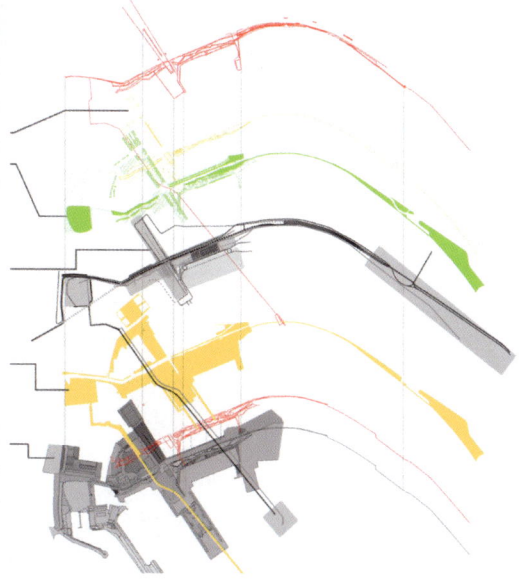

New Monumental Harbour in Naples, E.B.S.G., T-Studio - G. Salimei, 3C+T (F. Capolei, P. Capolei), R. Pavia, Ippozone, M. di Venosa, VIA Ingegneria, Naples, 2006-in progress.

The redevelopment project of the Monumental Port of Naples involves the interface area between the port and the city with the development of a complex urban project capable of connecting different parts of the sea front. The linking of the port's long perimeter to the city's landmark center involves the creation of a ground system called "filtering line", which will transform the separation into an exchange and correlation system between the city's resources and the port's by forging a strong link between the city's major sites and the various functional areas of the port. The system will be brought to completion through a ground conformation that, by incorporating urban and port activities in its variable section while nonetheless keeping them distinct, will extend from the future Parco della Marinella to the public park across from the Royal Palace, from Park to Park. As a linear system of areas equipped for services, cultural and commercial activities and public parks with pedestrian and cycling paths, it will become a great promenade paysagèe, providing the city and the port with all the facilities and services it needs.

New Monumental Harbour in Naples - molo Beverello, Naples, 2006-in progress.

criticizes the idea of an indefinitely extensible city, whose sole concern seems to be to expand to the point of bursting[15].

Extended to the more general problem of the existence of infrastructures which act as urban breaks and large fractures, the building-bridge, which is a kind of bridge-city, can become a powerful element of the urban imagination, which can reconcile even different scales and, in particular situations, rehabilitate old symbolic and metaphorical values, such as the gate of a city and of a district, the privileged ritual of urban theatricality and conviviality, an initiatory rite of passage. Above all, it can offer, in situations of decay, a significant means of modifying the surroundings.

The urbanized bridge is a symbol of the quality of urban life that needs to be reclaimed and revitalized. In this sense, the principle of the urbanized bridge as a new public place is dense with future potential.

A number of inhabited bridges that hover over a valley was Bernard Tschumi's answer to the condition of fracture that arose in the city of Lausanne, where an old industrial zone, located at a lower level than the rest of the city, was separated from the historic core and the other side of the city. Two bridges now cross the valley, connecting the two banks. Tschumi's idea was to impose a serial repetition of these elements along this part of the valley. These, reinterpreted in their bridge essence, were meant to be lived at multiple levels and in multiple

Ponte Vecchio, Florence (archive image)

Drawing La Ville Spatiale over the Hudson River, Yona Friedman 1964.

ways, not just as elements of transition but also as dwellings, inhabited bridges which as such relate the two parts of the city and the valley below, but which, above all, through their more complex structure, succeed in creating a sort of connective tissue, a system that encompasses both transport services and cultural, museum and entertainment facilities. These aerial elements, which become "connectors", as Tschumi defines them, weave a web of relationships that include a complexity of functions and make of these places a hub of attraction for the whole city.

Inhabited bridges that connect in this way two parts of a city, both vertically and horizontally, and allow various realities to communicate with each other through the use of treadmills, escalators, elevators and other devices. The upper part of these bridge-cities almost always continues to function as a passageway, primarily for vehicular traffic, while below they recreate a world

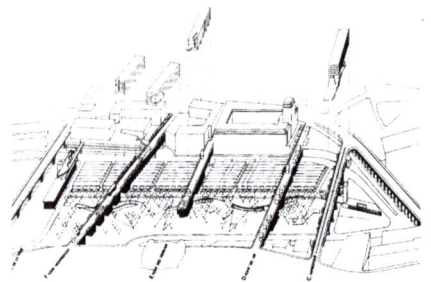

Bridge City, B. Tschumi, Lausanne 2002.

unto itself, portions of the city which can host a variety of activities and in which a complexity of spaces makes them a pleasant destination for leisure and entertainment.

Even a bus depot, a place of trade and traffic, linked to a rail network, an airport and maritime traffic, can become something else: a great square for relating. In Stockholm, a bridge-building, the Vasaterminalen, designed by Ralph Erskine, hovering over the area occupied by tracks, becomes, through its multiple functions, a place full of energy that acts as a great place for rendezvous and exchanges of culture and entertainment in the city center.

In an era in which travel has become increasingly dominant in our lives, a rendezvous center in the midst of this flux well interprets the possible transformation of urban public places, becoming the true square of the third millennium. Places for living are not divided, do not have a static connotation but become vectors of events which can be arranged so as to meet, collide and interact with each other and, above all, to discover that the result is of great interest for the development of our city 16.

Ralph Erskine's great bridge-building recreates within itself the very complexity of a city, alternating in its composition even different and at times isolable functions, as in the case of the World Trade Center, whose offices occupy the upper floors of the complex. All the areas of this bridge-building are structured around a large central reservoir and a pedestrian street facing offices, restaurants, shops, cafes and all the various activities that contribute to making this place a true urban setting. The whole space is unified by a large cascade roof that captures as much light as possible, almost reinterpreting in its form the kind of glass roofs found in 19th-century railroad stations, or better the kind of 19th-century urban arcades as a great urban metaphor.

This complex, conceived as a trade building, is interesting for its will to become something more. A large urban arcade, a place where one can stop and not just hurry by, a place where one can meet people, dine and at the same time shop and take part in various activities. The different sections are completely autonomous, coexist, interlace, and the intermingling is continuous. Yet they are in equilibrium: there is no subordination of the big glazed space of the arcade to the volume of the offices. It is an authentic city because its parts are autonomous and linked together, interfering with each other but without overbearing.

On the outskirts of Bern a great bridge-building, a multipurpose center, located above a highway, has become an icon in the landscape and at the same time a gateway to the city, an integral part of the great traffic artery. The building is large-scale, sculpturesque, designed to be viewed at high speed. It is an inhabited bridge (a Daniel Libeskind project) made up of a series of separate, disconnected segments that are joined to one another like the result of an overlapping of elements over time, so that the bridge almost seems added onto the bodies, or vice versa.

The impression is of an artificial, composed landscape. The roadside segments, actual bridge anchors whose irregular pattern, reminiscent of certain rock formations, is well-rooted in the surrounding area. The building houses services and entertainment spots such as a large swimming pool and gyms.

The suspended part, formed by a big "stage" on the Westside, is crossed by paths at various levels: a glass arcade from which we observe the whole surrounding landscape, the highway below included, and a pedestrian overpass, designed for quick crossing, that looks onto a large hall, a true square, an urban place for commerce and encounters where one can stop and not just rush by.

The space is complex and offers a variety of views from its terraces set at different levels and bordering on other pathways, to create unexpected spaces. The reference is to Piranesi's complex spatial designs and to the articulation of perspective views in constant motion which induces a flexibility of perception and use.

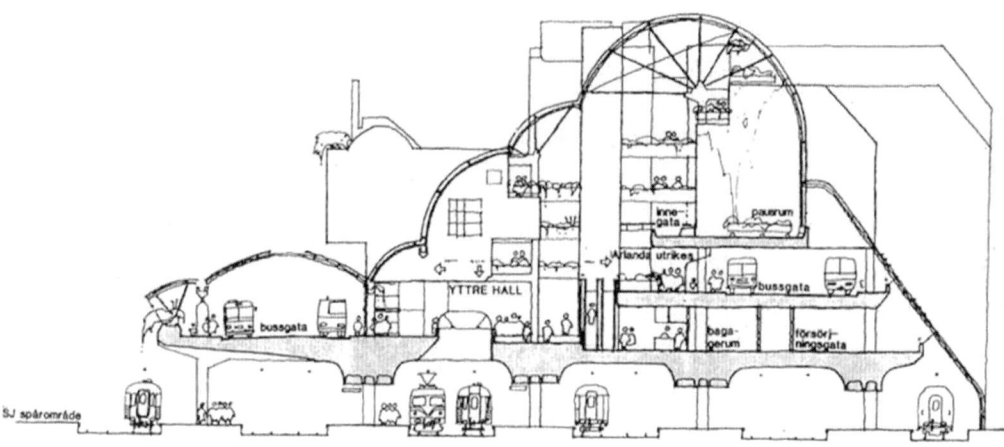

Vasa terminalen bus terminal, R. Erskine, Stockholm, 1989.

There are several unexpected pathways that form a membrane of public activities at various levels. The network of paths thus created does not have a linear pattern but a multivalent one, ready to generate a sense of adventure and excitement. It contains shops, cafes, and places for summer and winter recreation, distributed in a system of different sectors and pending events suspended over the street.

This complex occupies a unique position as an excellent interpretation of how to exploit this kind of infrastructure, offering a mechanism of urban growth composed of an overlap of meanings: an idea of urban construction whose dynamics have never been interrupted.

Pont Neuf, J.B. Raguenet, 1756, Paris.

The totem-building

Among the several expressions the great collective hubs can assume there is the special one of out-of-scale objects, which must be perceived from 360 degrees, often from across the city, as points of reference and authentic signals.

Some places, if located in especially extreme, peripheral or isolated situations, are more often than not perceived distractedly and on the run. To capture one's attention they must be able to concentrate their tensions into a sort of great urban sculpture which, precisely because of its out-of-scale character, often estranged from its context, acts as an energy catalyst. Often this powerful symbolic element refers to imaginary figures whose out-of-scale design transforms them into great charismatic images. Their unique strength resides in the ambivalence they express, the sense of ambiguity they transmit, characterized by their super-size image, a large element that houses

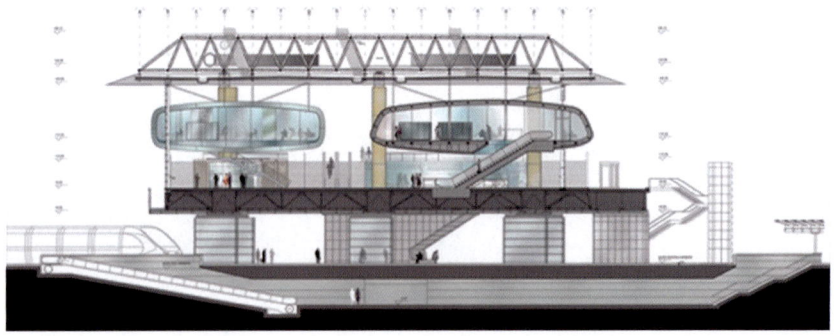

Tiburtina Station, Studio ABDR, Rome, 2006-2011.

Rome's new high-speed railroad station (which replaces the old the late 19th-century station), and an authentic arcade-bridge. Designed by Rome's ABDR Studio, it virtually and physically connects the two areas previously separated from the cluster of tracks. The arcade-bridge, entirely covered by a large steel and printed glass surface in various shades of color that produce a striking color pattern, is 300 meters long, with a 9-meter height above the tracks, contains ticket offices, services, bars, shops and restaurants, and has the form of a large square that, besides serving as a central point, must be able to connect the Nomentano and Pietralata districts.

a proliferation of events. So, if on the one hand they impinge on the metropolis with a monumental language, a powerful expression that must draw to itself all the dynamism of speed and a multiplicity of perceptions, on the other hand, the inside of these complexes conceals another world on a much more human scale, subtle and multi-faceted.

Their strength lies also in the very ambivalence which the best examples of these architectures express.

These super-sized places can accommodate a proliferation of events in a single large container. These containers, which look like enormous sculptures, embody a powerful tension between the needs of collective representation and those of individual freedom. The terse character of an exterior that dialogues with the world of the automobile in an extreme rapidity of fruition, through powerful, pithy, often compelling images, corresponds to a more secretive, more intimate inner space full of referential elements for "(...) those

Basilea Station, Cruz y Ortiz Arquitectos, Basilea, 2003.

The Basel Railroad Station, parallel to its tracks, presents the typical problems of any intermodal station, namely a strong break with the city. The proposed transformation would restore the important role of the urban infrastructures as entry point to the city for travelers who come and go, and as a link between outlying districts which have no direct connection. This problem was solved by building an elevated walkway with shops, services and cultural activities, and a large square overhead which, in addition to containing all the station facilities, serves as an excellent connection point between the two districts cut by the tracks, an inhabited bridge visible from different parts of the city. The shape of the roof is largely responsible for its renewed image, recalling the city skyline, and makes this bridge-passage a powerful feature for the city.

who look at the surrounding movement that has become the destiny of the contemporary city"[17].

The terse image of these large-scale objects conveys a particular force which is no longer the bearer of a sole message but of a dense cluster of messages, each of which in turn is subject to multiple interpretations. Often these objects belong simultaneously to two scales, and through the tension they generate, convey a sense of collective belonging similar to the valence of a totem[18].

As for their external urban character, these objects are built mainly on a giant scale. There are no significant variations in scaling, the aspect ratio measures itself prevalently against the city. The canonic tripartite division of the building, presumably rooted in the ground, with an intermediate part that represents it, and a final attachment to the sky, is often maintained, but the individual elements appear magnified, often out of proportion, above all free of any human-scale relationship. The eye must be able to store the message even in a distracted, casual way, and piece together the meaning of this architectural work while often ignoring its architectural details.

The situations in which these objects occur are of the most varied, from purlieus slums where these objects seem as strange as enormous spacecraft that have landed there by accident, to more standard situations where the object takes its cue from the urban context, or even, as in the case of Zeebrugge, where they stand completely outside of any urban context, thus becoming reference points for an entire area.

The large complex designed by Rafael Moneo that rises on the Diagonal, Barcelonas's main traffic artery, is located on the border between the urban fabric of the regular square blocks of the Cerdà district and the isolated buildings of the suburbs. The Diagonal, which has a character all its own in its interruption of the orthogonal grid, serving as a major high-speed traffic artery, but at the same time it is an important pedestrian axis, well-frequented at every point. The complex well interprets this thoroughfare situation by representing the big element of an out-of-scale city gate, which takes up several blocks, gathering all the irregularities of the city and placing them within its structure, to make them an integral part of its composition. The whole takes shape as a great building-city that has two very different faces representing the two urban realities of this part of the city. The complex features a marked duality between interior and exterior. Its main façade, looking towards the Diagonal, is a long street curtain that stretches compactly for a distance of three hundred meters, while inside, a large urban arcade opens onto a different, more human-sized intimate world.

The street side features slight recesses, designed not so much to be seen from vehicles speeding along the Diagonal, from which one barely notices the variations produced, as rather for its partial, foreshortened view, to be viewed by the pedestrians who use the structure, as a way of reducing its imposing monotony and severity by breaking up the façade into individual, isolated volumes.

The building is joined to the city by a series of underground floors used to provide services and above all a passageway and a parking area, the way a ship's hold is anchored to the sea. Its attachment to the ground has the shape of this huge ocean liner's foundation, consisting of a large black marble base interrupted by large glass windows. At night, when these shop windows are lighted, the base seems to dematerialize, a sensation that intensifies if one strolls briskly along the avenue. The window, as the only repeated element,

Zeebrugge sea terminal, OMA - Rem Koolhaas, Zeebrugge (Belgium), 1989.

gives unity to the whole front, but the long window wall imperceptibly changes its composition each time, as if to emphasize the slight changes in volume.

The great mass of white walls forms the main body of the building. Since it is punctuated by an obsessive series of openings, it cannot be perceived in its entirety, unless in passing or from afar, at great speed and distractedly, only as a texture of the material, the openings themselves becoming a design in the marble.

The long complex ends in a deliberate jaggedness, an irregular contour that seems to want to reproduce within the big block its composition by parts, a skyline sample of the city's heterogeneity. The whole to mitigate and lighten the dense view of the long façade that, once raised near the corners, in the instant of its dynamic view, is recomposed into a unitary element as a great city wall.

The arcade inside, which seems the combination of a large square or patio continually crossed by paths and a complex 19th-century passage, introduces us to a narrative itinerary that is articulated as a micro-cosmos, where large and small are brought up close and mixed together to ensure greater variety to the user, and where particular attention to the fragmentation of space, so important for the customization of goods, makes it a target for an uninterrupted mass of people. The interior of this complex reproduces the same features as its exterior. The great glass-covered square is lined with windows, and the travertine is the same as that used for the street façade. The whole merely reinforces the micro-cosmos, where the disorientation caused by the ambiguity of being continuously inside-outside is repeatedly present.

It is a new center of relations, where the need to respond to the demands of contemporary consumption is reconciled with the traditional utility spaces of our European cities. "The construction of the area will not be divided into separate parts but rather seeks to reinforce its singularity as a center of urban interest. This solution, which appears purely compositional, aims at producing a system of maximum public utility. The congruence of the area with the shape of the city will make it of extreme public interest, regardless of the uses to which may be put by spontaneous processes over time"[19].

The grandeur of this complex seems almost to defy time, especially if perceived at automobile or train speed; its external shape is affected by this vision, taking shape as an out-of-scale object.

In a particularly rundown London suburb, near a highway, next to a railway, lies a multipurpose complex designed by Ralph Erskine. Its appearance cannot fail to impress even the most hurried motorist or distracted rail passenger. Externally it looks like a large out-of-scale object, finished and fully defined,

Diagonal Complex, R. Moneo e M. de Solá Morales, Barcelona, 1993.

self-contained and isolated from the environment, where it stands out like a sore thumb, a blunt, peremptory image reminiscent of a fortress, a world apart, introverted, unknown, seemingly impenetrable but nonetheless perceivable from any direction.

Its attachment to the ground is a great foundation, a solid wall marked by four massive pillars, in the shape of buttresses, their masonry treated with a special brick pattern which makes them even more striking. The main body, a spiral that flares upward, is surrounded by horizontal glass bands alternately opaque and transparent, placed at the necessary height to allow people, whether seated or standing, to look outside. These bands, interspersed with a copper element, a kind of iridescent material, widen and unravel, ceasing on the south side to allow large windows to open. The large curved roof, partially openable, resting on the building like a large carpet, thins and frays to give way to the brick pillar structure and large glass surfaces, which illuminate the central space. From this rises a series of elements, sculpture-objects, strange chimneys, like the pipe-unions of ships that capture additional light and air. The last, the highest, is a kind of tower, an all-glass turret which offers a stunning view of London. The Ark has a space that is not easy to describe; the best way is to experience entering it; it is essential to let oneself go to the discontinuous and readable, multi-directional narrative: walking at random inside this unreal realm promises continual discoveries and varied happenings. It is a space full of tension, suggestive, which can be experienced in many ways, prepared to serve multiple functions; a series of small worlds where concerts, exhibitions and conferences can take place, and where there are restaurants, two floors of parking areas, and more. A place, in short, where one can linger; almost a complete spatially rich container, but to be completed each time by experiencing it; "it is a territory to colonize, a territory of artificial nature"[20]. The Hammersmith Ark was founded on the idea of transforming a place into a center for communication, and, like Noah's Ark, it is a refuge, an alternative to the environmental chaos of its surroundings, therefore, a city within a city.

Placing a great landmark in a very odd landscape suspended between sea and land is a rather singular enterprise: the construction of a ferry terminal as an alternative to the Channel Tunnel. The OMA project opts for a form that resists easy classifications and suggests, through successive associations, the mechanical, the industrial, the utilitarian, the abstract, the poetic, the surreal, and tries to react with the loftiest artistry and maximum efficiency.

The idea was to create a great Tower of Babel that, unlike the mythical model of ambition transformed into a symbol of powerlessness in the face of events,

LM Harbor gateway,
S. Holl, Copenhagen, 2008-in progress.

Steven Holl's project for an access totem to the Port of Copenhagen stands as an iconic landmark for the city and was realized with the design of two tall towers which in turn are connected to two bridges that form a pedestrian walkway at 65 meters above the harbor. These buildings, joined in a kind of embrace, are a symbolic gateway to the city from the sea. The project, which uses a variety of sustainable solutions, such as an alternative energy system generating electricity with turbines that draw in port water, is a kind of beacon, and in the words of S. Holl himself [...] "this project comprises a several-storied building, which links the city together and works as a point of reference in the harbor."

Torre de Gas Natural, Studio EMBT – E. Miralles e B. Tagliabue, La Barceloneta, Barcellona, 2007.

is a model of ergonomic efficiency, a centrifuge that gathers travelers from all over Europe, entertains them, reinvigorates them with its multiple possibilities, and sorts them towards their various destinations.

The building has a very particular and fascinating shape, determined by the intersection of a vertical element similar to an obelisk, a signal capable of attracting attention by its elongated and upward-tending form, and of a sphere, a highly receptive element, thanks to its extreme ability to absorb within its volume multiple objects, events, people and symbols. The shape effectively expresses the duality of this large container which, on the one hand, in a spiral towards the top, with a centrifugal movement, and on the other, through its outer tentacles captures all possible forms of expression and movement, circumscribing them in one place and encompassing them within it in a hollow space, a micro-city possessing a number of autonomous possibilities and activities, all under a great cap from which one can enjoy a view both skywards and earthwards, the latter where the parking areas and the various sorting areas are located. Its compact, uniform, unitary shape, a great shell, like a giant octopus, becomes a signal that communicates to the outside an event visible from a distance; a large-scale image that can be sighted from the sea and from the flat surrounding countryside as a point of reference: a crossroads of various possible directions.

The great object, dotted with openings that allow views of the surrounding landscape framing the horizon in a radius of 360°, rests on the ground abstractly, through a series of pylons that seem temporary elements of support, a kind of scaffolding that props it up pending the takeoff or landing of a monstrous spacecraft, which leaves to walkways, ramps and roads the task of establishing contact between the building's interior and the outside world.

Inside there is a self-contained world that unfolds in all its daily components of lingering, working, traveling; an artificial world that becomes a gathering place characterized by fluid, dynamic spaces that can be traversed and experienced in different ways in different seasons and at different times of day. Their stratification in horizontally and always differently stacked levels creates conflicts by drawing variously characterized shapes and areas, as normally occurs in a real city, where buildings flank, intersect and overlap each other to gain space for themselves in the city.

Apropos of Erskine's Ark, the terminal's shape, abstraction and smooth continuous surface skin make the building's static reading impossible and suggest a principle of dynamism.

These large urban sculptures invite us to observe, to enter something animate, unfinished, in perennial transformation, and offer different levels of interpretation of an existence constantly shifting between a need for encounter and a desire for pause. These, on the one hand, reproduce the city as a lifeline for work, commerce and culture, and on the other satisfy a desperate need for individual activities, places where we can experience inner events, act out our emotional fantasies; in short, a place where we can live out even the most hidden, subjective aspect of our age[21]. In Amsterdam's harbor Renzo Piano has constructed Metropolis, a building suspended between land and water, above the entrance to an underwater automotive tunnel. By completely incorporating the expressway which passes through the port, the building accentuates its dynamic capacity, reinterpreting the shape of a ship's bow in concrete, copper and glass, and by organizing a complex system with several functions; it becomes a landmark-building for the entire port. The building, thanks to its location, resolves a particularly articulated node consisting of two powerful elements, the road network and the sea, and is emphatically marked by two crossings: one for pedestrians, a broad flight of steps that leads directly to the museum entrance; the other a driveway which enters the building and crosses the harbor to reach the opposite shore.

In a context featuring such a powerful horizontal dimension as the city of Amsterdam, the originality of the building lies in its three-dimensionality, thanks to the tiered square overlooking the sea from a height of three meters. Its ship-like form makes it easy to collocate it as an integral part of the harbor. The elevated square becomes a sort of Agora, a lookout place for commerce, encounters and communication. The Center hosts permanent exhibitions on energy, technology and communication. Inside there is free access to computers connected to the internet, and it is in this sense that the project finds its equilibrium with the port, in its capacity for commerce and communication.

The Forum of architects Herzog & de Meuron, in Barcelona, is a triangular building that extends horizontally at the top of the new Esplanada that in connecting the Diagonal to the sea favors the natural confluence of pedestrians both within it and on the square.

The Forum triangle is well-connected to the rest of the city by a metro line and a new tram line, and looks almost like a suspended block whose broad sloping terrain is grafted onto the building to form, along with it, a large outdoor public space or arena. Its access point is a large ground-floor entrance, which is a beckoning element to a variety of activities, among which an events hall that can contain up to 4,000 people, as well as multi-functional spaces. Repeated skylight cuts admit light, linking the inner and outer sections of the square in an odd ambience in precarious equilibrium between interior and exterior.

The covered area beneath the triangular surface is shaped as a hybrid space: an urban square which is a meeting place; a public place where a series of patios intersect the elevated structure and establish a complex interaction between open and covered spaces and the various levels of the Forum headquarters, constantly creating new perspectives and unusual lighting effects.

The Ark, R. Erskine, Hammersmith, London, 1992.

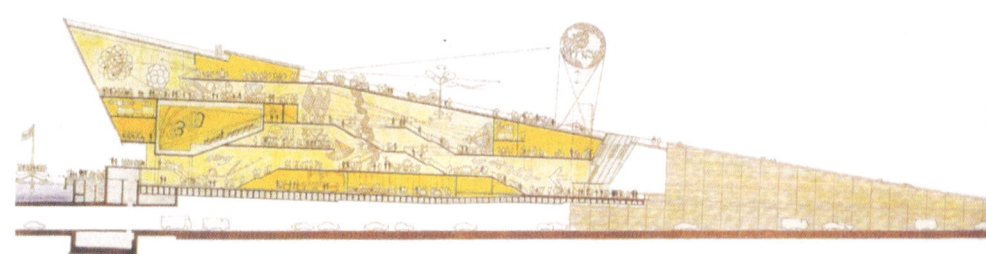

NEMO (National Center for Science and Technology), Renzo Piano Building Workshop, Amsterdam, the Netherlands 1997.

176

Chapter 4

The arcade-building

By virtue of its structure which makes it possible to connect spaces, activities and varied functions, the arcade may become the backbone of the new public places, the signal identifying element of the urban setting.

Harking back to the aggregating role of its predecessors, the monumental arcades of the 20th century, today's arcades serve as a connecting and revitalizing element of complex urban situations, to become a sort of ordering principle of differences, commerce, communication, flux and the most varied situations. They are often given the shape of a public place, but, in a more decisive way than the street itself, they manage to create in their interiors occasions for encounter, relaxation and leisure. Their interiors are large, hosting a constant play of contrasting sensations that create a strong sense of ambiguity and disorientation. We have the impression of being in an outside which is really an inside, an interior shaped like an exterior, a space experienced as empty, while in contrast to the city it is actually full, that is to say open but at the same time closed. It is often privately owned but within the city plays an eminently public role.

In effect, the role it plays at the urban level is often strategic: it is an element that connects parts of the city, an element that historically has always belonged to the city and becomes a fulcrum, a point which absorbs and radiates energy, a nucleus of activity and a structure of complexity that become its soul, the greatest force of attraction of the whole project. It is derived to some extent from the passage but is a more imposing structure. The arcade is often formed by a very high roof that is perceived by the city and acts as a signal. The passage, on the contrary, had a more secretive character. The arcade is sunnier, less to discover, often its armature is less hidden and the sensation of a maze of streets, characteristic of the passages, becomes a stroll under an open sky. Actually the arcade as such still conserves a great sense of ambiguity and indeterminacy; in passing through it one still has a sense of disorientation, for the façades are equivalent to external ones, the windows continue to face inward onto a large interior, and precisely because of its flexible nature as a covered vacuum, which is a relationship between things: it is an indeterminate structure, in continual evolution, which relates to different situations and is continually renewable The more natural the connection of buildings of different forms and periods within a great unifying element that can embrace and develop everything, the more this will become the heart of the project and the street will become an important point for encounters and a flow of energy, not only confirming its role as a place of transit but enriching its functions and potential.

This is the case of Zeppelinstrasse, which on crossing the May Center block in Cologne becomes a new arcade where the attempt is to bring together different elements and situations, such as an old building, another newly constructed one, and a street.

Connecting the two blocks helps convince passersby to stop and stay. They become an attraction for the entire city, a place for experiencing new sensations, and a true arcade-building. The arcade, while maintaining the character of a public street, with its role as a transit point between the city and public space, makes it possible to carry out multiple tasks and functions that attract larger crowds than those from transit alone.

The Olivandehof Arcade maintains the character of the street and so reaffirms its role as a transit point between the city and a public space and becomes what we have identified as an arcade-building, in which a series of catwalks, besides making further connections within the arcade itself, connect the two contiguous blocks.

From the purely urban arcade we pass on to another empty space in the form of a large elliptical atrium. Both have a gray-green colored steel structure that is continually interrupted by transparent escalators, which, through their constant movement, provoke a sensation of fluidity, a live element, almost a beating heart, a kind of lifeline that connects all the levels and makes them live in continuous connection. Its elliptical shape, which recalls the layout of certain historic squares, is functional and gives a sensation of warmth, protection; yet this is immediately contradicted by the fact that it too is an empty, completely open space; we can just look out, or stroll through it on the escalators or the various all-glass escalators or elevators, which offers a view of this continuous flux.

The many escalators and the transparent elevator that cross the atrium form a rather surreal space where the racing of the stairs is accentuated by the fact that, as these are transparent, they are reflected in each other, and their blue show-through internal mechanism makes them seem very airy and light. All this helps recreate an atmosphere typical of the most famous paintings of Escher, where interminable flights of stairs pursue each other in a maze which is an evident impossibility.

Fórum Building, Herzog & de Meuron, Barcelona, 2004.

The atrium and the arcade are covered by a large glass window that diffuses the light without the need for a mechanism to shield against the sun's rays, since we are in a climate like that of Cologne, where public spaces seem to be in constant search of light.

There is a sharp contrast between the heavy pre-existence in stone and the light structures of the roof of the actual arcade, the steel walkways and the atrium, which is also covered over by a transparent steel roof.

A particular urban situation that encloses a piece of the city's history are the two skyscrapers designed and manufactured by S.O.M., Skidmore Owings and Merrill, which coexist with buildings of only four or five stories. Two worlds, interacting with each other, touch each other, collide, ignore each other and generate an interstitial space: a leftover space.

Calatrava's answer to the problem is this transformation into a great urban arcade, a great catalyst for this whole heterogeneity. The arcade, in its white abstractness, seen through a vertical space that tends to free itself upwards as if to capture light, mimics the shape of a tree-lined avenue, and the interweaving of the roof's vaulted structures produces a compact design, a play of lights and shadows which, in projecting itself onto the inner buildings, diffuses throughout, giving us the pleasant and at the same time disquieting sensation of being covered by the dappling of tree foliage on the great windows and on the glass-concrete floor, which conveys the light through to the floors below.

The arcade as a great urban boulevard has the function of connecting two parts of the city; it becomes a place of transition but also of shelter and encounter, recalling by its special shape the belly of a whale or a large vertebrate; it brings us together, providing a sense of protection. It takes us to a world apart, where the fundamental idea is to transform a completely secondary, unprivileged, leftover space into a public meeting place. Just as the Gothic cathedrals, through their upward momentum, indicated a certain dynamism, so this place propels us into a circulation and transformation of energy that leads us into a space that envelops us in a new body and invents a series of new suggestions, forcing us to pass through it and experience all its perspectives, discover different effects and unexpected reflections, both at different times of day and in different seasons. The observer, as in the Gothic cathedrals, is forced to pass through it up to where the arcade finds a point of stasis in a square broadening, a kind of pause, a point where the forces are gathered and concentrated. This point is the project's fulcrum: here the

Gallery of My Zeil Shopping Center, Studio Fuksas, Frankfurt am Main, 2009.

Massimiliano Fuksas' *MyZeil* is a new shopping center located in the center of Frankfurt. The project is inspired by the canyon-like landscape, and the heart of the building is a large vertical arcade which looks onto six floors of activities related to commercial and refreshment activities. A series of long escalators plow the big empty space, creating a variety of exceptional views that call to mind the bizarre mazelike images of Piranesi's Prisons. The strong point of this great gallery is the roof, funnel-shaped with triangular glass panels connected together by metal elements of different sizes, which spans the entire height, creating special lighting effects inside the building.

idea is of a small grove with a dense interweaving of branches, leaves, light and shadow, where the energy arrives, and in a play of spirals and pillars that have more than one direction and pursue each other in a new, original space, a covered-uncovered, indoor-outdoor, closed-open, inside-outside arcade-square.

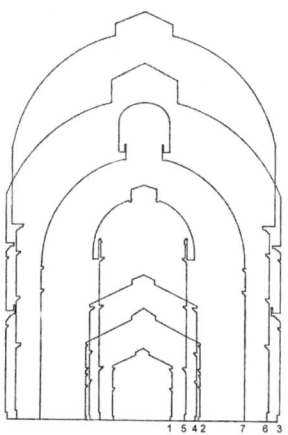

Passage, Paris

Comparative diagram of the cross sections of the main European Galleria (based on: Geist J. F., *Le passage*, Paris, 1982)

1. Paris, Galleria Vivienne, 1825
2. Paris, Galleria Colbert, 1826
3. Milan, Galleria Vittorio Emanuele, 1867
4. Berlin, Kaisergalerie, 1873
5. La Haye, Passage, 1885
6. Naples, Galleria Umberto I, 1891
7. Berlin, Friedrichstrasse, 1908

Galleria BCE, S. Calatrava, Toronto, 1994.

Olivandenhof gallery, Hetrich-Petschnigg & Partner (HPP), Cologne, 1988.

NOTES

1 Interview to J.Nouvel in «Domus», May 2010.
2 Frampton 1980.
3 The project of RKW radically rethink the center and revitalize it. The solutions come from the idea of inserting a great cover that protects from the atmospheric agents, There was the introduction of a glass roof covering all shopping arcades. It created a different spatiality, where the connection of functions and areas is resolved by a large urban galleria.
4 Tschumi 2005.
5 This hypothesis of classification concerns the mode of existence of a particular architectural space through the theoretical elaboration of its elementary or basic parameters. Ugo 1991.
6 Ugo 1991.
7 Alberti 1466.
8 Rykwert 1972.
9 Ugo 1991.
10 Filarete 1464.
11 "If Leoh Ming Pei's glass pyramid adds a memorable form to the urban architectural lexicon, its entrance seems all wrong. Wedged between the long wings of the Louvre along with two smaller glass pyramids, it appears as a monumental description of the great Freudian phobia of the vagina dentata; a more voluptuous mons veneris would have been more appropriate. But once inside the great subterranean uterus, we discover a new space and a captivating movement. Visiting a museum today, which includes purchasing books, posters and postcards, and a stop at the restaurant and perhaps seeing a film, has become strangely like visiting a shopping center. At the Grand Louvre the similarity becomes explicit through the addition of a luxurious shopping mall connected to the underground entrance as the museum's backdoor, using as its icon a capsized glass pyramid. Here, the mixture of the subway, shops, restaurants and spaces for the fashion industry's annual show, has been added to the museum's program, creating a wealth of possibilities for social contact to and the awareness of a different reality, even if the fashion industry is the historic progenitor of consumerism." Ingersoll 1996, p. 122.
12 Seppilli 1977.
13 "What is a constructed thing?" Heidegger wondered. "An example – a bridge – will help our effort to think. 'Light and powerful ', the bridge hovers above the river. It does not limit itself simply to connecting two pre-existing banks. It is actually the very passage of the bridge that reveals the banks as such. It unites the river, its banks and the surrounding territory. The bridge gathers the area around the river as a region. It is a place." The bridge gathers the scattered elements of nature in its Simmelian separateness and transforms the indeterminate space-extension of the territory into a definite place through the construction, itself (as demonstrated by the etymology of the verb bauen) about to be. "Constructing is part of living, and receives from this its being (wesen). It is, in its being, "allowing to inhabit". Realizing the being of constructing is the building of places by gathering their spaces. It is only when we can inhabit that we can build. Inhabiting is the fundamental character of being (sein)." Ugo 1991, pp. 186-187.
14 Bridge and Door: two elements in which "the will to connect becomes the shape of things. In the construction of a bridge, this effort reaches its apex. Here it is not only the passive separation which is characteristic of space, but also an active, specific configuration, that seems to oppose the human will to unite. By overcoming this obstacle, the bridge symbolizes an expansion of the sphere of our will over space. The bridge becomes an aesthetic value when it completes the union of separateness in so effectual a way as to absolve its practical finalities, but also when it makes it immediately apparent. It has, with the banks it unites, a much closer and less fortuitous relationship than subsists between a house and its land and foundations, which are hidden beneath it. Simmel's text thus confirms what we have said. "If for the bridge – he goes on to say – the phases that relate to separation and connection behave in such a way that the former seems to belong to nature, while the latter to mankind, with the door both penetrate in the same measure into human action, mankind's action". Simmel 1909, pp. 4-6.
15 "It seems to mean overlapping, a juxtaposing of signs stratified in history or in the metaphorical values that accompany the bridge idea itself". Gregotti 1991, p. 9
16 Dethier 1991.
17 Hence the need for the architect not to divide the places of urban space into static (the block and the building) and dynamic (the street), but to consider them all as bearers of events and therefore to have them meet and collide with each other, on the actually optimistic assumption that this will produce new occasions and therefore knowledge and progress." Ingersoll 1993, p. 57.
18 The façade, for example, during the Baroque era had a direct, predominant role in constructing the urban setting, and was primarily designed to be perceived on long axes, or obliquely, from a given perspective, and in any case was

Chapter 4

conceived for scenic views on foot and often favored a single point of observation. Today, the role of the façade has changed; there is no privileged model of perception; a building can be experienced in full or only in some of its parts, and our perception, based on speed and the means employed, no longer determines a geometrically continuous and identifiable space, so much as a dynamic succession of images and signals. Above all, a building, in no longer presenting a main façade and lesser sides, is considered in its entire form, often without having a hierarchically more important element that is its public mask. And so the appropriation of urban space always comes about more through the expression of the building's parts or fragments.
19 Lucan 1993.
20 Secchi R. 1991.
21 Pousse 1995.

Chapter 5

5 The characters of a new language coming into being

> **❝** *If modernism recognized itself as a project of opposition and post-modernism in the word recomposition, today we can speak of transposition, where by transposition we mean a process of migration which involves contamination, a kind of reconciliation of opposites. A process of mixing things and events, words and people, of renaming effects and phenomena, where "everything is transposed into another hybrid and intermediate and approximate, interrupted, contaminated and separate".* **❞**

(F. Purini)

The Tower of Babel, Pieter Bruegel the Elder, 1563.

The characters of a new language coming into being

Franco Purini offers a metaphor by which he identifies the public space as an architectural language, arguing that its current features have a wealth of possibilities and potentials[1].

In a certain sense the public space can interpret a wider range of movements and expressions, and indeed architectural language can no longer be identified as a corpus that carries with it the notions of finiteness, uniqueness, which implies a certain sacral sentiment inspired by the duo uniqueness-identity. Continuing to consider it as a corpus will not get us to bring its factors of definition and constituent features to a crisis point. The structure of architectural language, in becoming a metaphor of public spaces, is enriched with complexity and freedom, potential and those features that predominate precisely in real public spaces.

This metaphor may help us get some useful insights into the significance of the expressions of these two values: architectural language and public space. This comparison offers a possible interpretation of such statutory problems. For example, what here (to stick with Purini's definition) we call public space is configured as a space of passage, yet more as a space of repose, a place to inhabit, but also, one hopes, to oppose and overturn in its established uses.

The characters that define the public space are no longer what they once were. The public use of space is a necessary but not sufficient requisite: public space seems rather one that hosts certain public functions endowed with a representative quality, which we can freely accede to and where functions are carried out in which the community puts itself on stage as such[2].

Another important factor that makes a space recognizable as a public space is the presence of a certain architectural quality that must have a relevant formal force and a certain capacity to take on a centralizing role.

Architectural language is a normally acceptable system of principles as a carrier of contents and common values. If modernism identified itself as opposition and post-modernism recognized itself in the word recomposition, today we can speak of transposition, where by transposition we mean a process of migration which involves contamination, a kind of reconciliation of opposites. In a process of mixing things and events, words and people, of renaming effects and phenomena, "everything is transposed into another hybrid and intermediate and approximate, interrupted, contaminated and separate"[3].

City of Fashion and Design, Jakob + Mac Farlane, Paris, 2008.

Euralille, J. Nouvel, - Lille, 1995.

This is an era that no longer pits opposites against each other, as happened in the recent past: city against countryside, plan against project, but rather sensitizes about the need for reconciliation.

The process of transposition identified by Purini is the product of different languages, of everyone's desire to find his own linguistic or ethnic group within a great container such as (to make a historical-geographical comparison) Europe.

Architectural language must surely go beyond the categories of orthodoxy, autonomy and philology, yet perhaps it must not turn into its opposite, but must be able to incorporate within it all possible variations.

Veles and Vents - America's Cup Building, D. Chipperfield, Valencia, 2007.

Real City (project), P. Cook, Frankfurt, 1986.

It is a language which, precisely because it is made up of a multiplicity of languages, different expressions, and mutations and a plurality of meanings, becomes an accurate expression and interpretation of the character of public places.

And like real languages, so the architecture of public places has its dialects, its specific characters, its well-defined areas, and absorbs these features, which take part in the phenomenon of mingling, as before mentioned, and help promote the freedom and autonomy of each context in relation to others. This leads to new possibilities of expression, new potentialities which arise also from the unexpected, unpredictable, not completely controlled nature of these mixtures. Having several alien, not completely understood factors react together leads to unexpected results which, as we have seen, contain doses of non-control. And this holds true for all the design elements of public places.

A language that no longer transmits definite, stable values is one that has a predominantly emotional and visual quality linked much more to sensory perceptions and emotional experiences.

All the elements of these complex projects, precisely because, as has been said many times, they tend to become autonomous objects with a life of their own, are likely to favor this emotional contact which tends more and more to be total, completely satisfying, even if each of them – as we shall see – corresponds to a specific universe.

This need has become even more necessary and indispensable today since we live in an era that is tending towards a marked artificiality and an extensive mechanization, and that, consequently, stimulates more sensorial-type reactions, and the desire to react to different factors and to obtain unforeseen, unexpected, not fully calculated results. Even the quest for all we do not know, which is alien to us, and the desire to contaminate, mix, confuse in order not to reveal its origin is, in this light, a direct expression of this interpretation[4].

The façade and its double

The façade, as the main front which contains an entrance and faces a street or square of some importance, has undergone varying styles in the course of architectural history, with varying degrees of autonomy and prominence, until the age of rationalist architecture, when buildings were designed with multiple outer fronts and the façade, as only one of these outer surfaces delimiting the building, became just one of the elements of a unitary object, and not necessarily the dominant one.

The façade, which has always had a direct role in the construction of the urban setting, was designed prevalently to be perceived along central axes, or obliquely, on a passing glance, and in any case was always conceived in a scenic rapport for viewing on foot. Today, our perception of a façade is also related to speed and is no longer a geometrically continuous and identifiable space, but rather a dynamic succession of images and signals. Hence the appropriation of urban space takes place today through the expression of fragments.

Something really new is taking place in contemporary architecture, characterized by the multiple possibilities it has of receiving and transmitting different meanings. As a result, all the parts of a building can contribute to this polyphony, no longer being constrained by a single meaning and not having to support a predetermined role, or having to have a consequent relationship of dependency with each other and with each to the whole. And here we refer not so much to a concept that analyzes the compositional aspect, but rather to the meaning this new viewpoint acquires.

In this light the façade, in some cases we might call it a building's surface or skin, can detach itself from the whole and live its own life; it has its own autonomy, which, as we have said, does not concern merely its form but mainly its meaning. This implies that the façade, in its role as mask, can receive, acknowledge and communicate differently from its interior, or disappear without compromising the very existence of the building or be incorporated inside its very shell, or configure itself in yet other expressions.

Surface is one of the key themes of this new architecture of public spaces in the contemporary city. Above all it is one of its possible modes of expression, one of the characters in which it can manifest different languages and express issues that interpret a plurality of views and where what we have identified as essential themes of public spaces, but in general central issues of all contemporary architecture, mainly manifest themselves. A building's surface becomes the physical location most suitable for representing ambivalence; the point where

Arab World Institute (detail of the façade), J. Nouvel, Paris, 1987.

the information system and the urban system interact, and where a building's communicative and symbolic content comes to grips with the need for a new identity of place and a renewed spatial and aesthetic quality.

The surface is free to dialogue with the context; it is free to affirm in itself its own conceptual content.

"Every façade, in the words of J. Nouvel, must respond to a theme, which in turn is part of an overall concept, the foundational concept of the project"[5].

It can also be an individual part in contrast to a context that contains the characters of formlessness and that can suggest nothing but an attitude of detachment. The façade is one of the elements that make up architecture, and it can bend itself to concepts, to vocabulary, to a site, and yet, in this context, retain a high degree of autonomy.

From the consideration that the façade is the countenance of the city, it follows that in these complex buildings, which in a way represent the city, the

Sendai Mediatheque, T. Ito, Senday, Japan, 1995.

façade takes on an even more complex role, becoming the boundary between an inner-outer, which of course is also an outer-inner and represents the transition between one world and another. Precisely because of this condition of ambivalence it becomes an urban transmitter of messages. The façade, as an element that has its immediate visibility, as an element that communicates with the outside world, may present particular signs, and these can become a very effective tool of communication. They communicate at once through their image and can also be continually renewed; hence they are transient, ephemeral, temporary, an aesthetic peculiarity of our time.

In this respect glass enables a wide range of expression, in its transparency and opacity, its depth and surface, and especially through the various processes it can undergo, from serigraphy to sanding and overlays, all of which make it possible to obtain special plays of light, shadow and reflection, which transform glass into a kind of fabric with its own warp and weave.

University library, W. Arets, Utrecht, 2004.

In other instances, the combination between screen and green is an element that acts as an interspace or filter between the inner-outer which softens and decides what to filter from the outside; for example, bamboo plants, interposed as interspace between the outside and the inside, also function as an ecological filter.

Sometimes the façade may no longer exist at all, or rather, there may be something that works in opposition to the façade, such as in the work of the group of Site Architects, with their wall concept: a filter that takes in and transmits information, whose meanings it gathers and returns in an ongoing game of give and take. The walls or partitions become phases of transition, passages of a sort, which tend and dissolve the traditional relationships between inner and outer by incorporating in itself their narrative comments. It is the walls that contain the information that constitute the elements of earth and soil, rising, passing through and falling again6.

Walls are like passages and can be a project challenge by offering themselves as transition lines in space; they can monitor the conditions of social and environmental change and interpret the stimuli that originate in society, the external environment, topography or their territory, something that comes from somewhere else that is not from the wall.

La Defence office complex, UN studio, Almere (the Netherlands), 2004.

Torre Agbar, J. Nouvel, Barcelona, 2005.

Quai Branly Museum (detail of the façade), J. Nouvel, Paris, France, 2006.

Chapter 5

Selfridges Centre, Future Systems, Birmingham, Great Britain, 2003.

Galleria Hall West, UNStudio, Seoul, South Korea, 2004.

Nature and artifice

The difference between nature and artifice tends to vanish. Just as human beings are coming more and more to resemble a receiving device, so buildings are coming more and more to resemble robots, subjects endowed with life, sensors, decision-making skills, ultimately resembling near-thinking beings. The relationship between nature and artifice at the dawn of the new millennium tends more and more towards integration, exchange of roles. As has been repeatedly pointed out, the great containers tend increasingly to incorporate natural elements, sensations and emotions related to nature.

The dual desire that these public places express is on the one hand to insert within them bits of nature, strips of landscape, in an attempt to recreate a true fragment of the city, together with natural elements; and on the other by the desire to offer sensations, impressions, emotions and spaces of nature proper, reinterpreting them as elements of architecture by making use of original elements which are the archetypes of the natural world, in order subsequently to transform them.

The inclusion of trees, plants, water, rocks and sand has become a constant in these public places. As major polarizers of leisure they contain entire portions of nature: lakes, trees, rivers, forests, fields. These artificial landscapes, rather than utilizing natural fragments as ornaments or purely literal transpositions, tend to be actual reproductions of nature, imitating sounds, colors and scents. The idea of including natural elements in these places was to reproduce the almost entirely lost proximity to nature which once so characterized urban life but which by now has all but disappeared as a result of globalization; and thus buildings tend to encompass within themselves the entire vocabulary of the city and the public space, such as streets, squares, markets, bridges, façades, soils and gardens.

The other aspect of the relationship between nature and artifice is revisitation, reinterpretation and re-signification of the raw elements of nature, which through a process of appropriation and endowment with new meanings, uses and forms, become a kind of artificial nature, without accomplishing a mere imitation or literal translation, but intervening with an architecturalizing of nature, or rather of the natural landscape.

The intent is to reinsert in architectural design the sensation of landscape and certain landscape archetypes, original models of nature, such as forests, gardens, glades, forms that relate more directly and intensely to our discipline.

Urban scenes in the Guzel-Hisar caravanserai, Turkey, 1836.

Headquarters of Champagne Piper et Heidsieck, J. Ferrier Architectures, Reims, 2008.

Chapter 5

California Academy of Sciences, R. Piano, San Francisco, 2008.

Gregotti maintains that the constitution of landscape as the configuration of a voluntary geography which offers itself as a significant image of the environment in which we move, leads to the recognition and assumption of the world as raw material re-elaborated by architecture through the invention of landscape as a whole[7].

The force of architecture, as Vittorio Ugo states, lies not in providing images but places, and so making reference to archetypes does not tend to offer literary or utopian images of nature but to create forms to start from and understand[8].

Several attempts at artificialization have been made in architecture, reinterpretations of natural phenomena, of the sensations that occur in nature. The forest, the first of these elements, may be perceived in two ways: either through the scientific detachment of cartography, or through a tactile, emotional involvement which experiences it from the inside, like a maze, as a primordial element in which we lose ourselves and are surrounded by a plethora of presences. This emotion is reinterpreted and artificialized, for example, in the structure of the hypostyle hall.

The second archetype Vittorio Ugo identifies is the garden, whose elements or parts belong to the universe of artifice, with their syntax and structural organization. The garden is by definition a natural form that is controlled, well-behaved and well-schooled, and is identified in some way with the home, an artifact endowed with its own order, therefore placing itself as median analogue between the micro and the macro cosmos, between the individuality of man and the totality of the world.

The third archetypal element is the glade, which is an absence, a void, a place opposed to the generic quantitative extension of space; an island, an oasis, a lake, something that is at the center of a small universe of artifice.

Heavy and light

In the past, an object, as Enzo Manzini says, had a meaning, told a story that seemed to come from the depths of the object itself, from the intimate identity of the materials of which it was composed, from the value placed on certain finishes, from its physical presence in three-dimensional space. What one saw was firmly etched into this quantum of material[9].

In the past, a material corresponded to a very specific use, and especially the birth, history and evolution of that material was clearly known, and it originated in the same order of magnitude and fell back into its sensory

Fünf Höfe Gallery Herzog and de Meuron, Münich, 1994-2003.

In the heart of Münich, a few hundred yards from the Marienplatz, the Swiss architects Herzog and de Meuron have reorganized a network of passages and courtyards. The Fünf Höfe is a system of five courtyards linked together which, although each has its own character, create a magical atmosphere delightful for strolling and, as Walter Benjamin suggested, losing one's way. There is a sharp contrast between the inside and the outside, for while the exteriors are completely in harmony with the historic 19th-century stone building, the interior is dominated by the color green, with giant ivy vines over ten yards long hanging from the ceiling, and by iron and glass materials. Inside you there is a network of contemporary passages, lively day and night, and interspersed with parking areas and plaza-like spaces with shops, restaurants, cafes and art galleries featuring renowned works such as Olafur Eliasson's Sphere

sphere. Now the evolution of material regards spaces and times it takes some effort for us to imagine but which we certainly cannot frequent. What in fact emerges and presents itself to our senses is, for us, something that seems to come from afar.

Today there is not only the utilization of elements with opposite characteristics through the mixture and fusion of heavy and light, opaque and transparent, glossy and translucent; but there is also an interesting quest for new materials with increasingly particular, studied and artificially produced features. And the interest lies increasingly in making them react together, in using them differently from how they originated, giving them in the end new life, use and potential.

We can speak of a mixed, continually contaminated language that incorporates all possible differences and re-elaborates them; in this sense one feels the need to identify certain key, recurring features, showing which can speak of a new way of understanding a language or several languages together, depending on which would seem more appropriate, given the existence of great, multiple differences between them.

There is also the frequent use of reflecting materials, or rather reflecting membranes, which are used to coat other materials and which act as dematerializing elements, dissolving or redoubling, and which, as it were, indicate several paths and not just one, since with their reflective properties they ensure that the visions are multiple and the images endless.

The labyrinthine space

The labyrinthine space is one where a person must lose himself, where he can lose his sense of direction, which has no hierarchies but proceeds with an infinite number of variations, devoid of duality gaps.

It is a space with the narrative structure of an open story, a place where one can wander towards a goal that is intuited but indeterminate. The labyrinthine space proposes the randomness and the complex, articulated weave of the old city, a feature particular to Mediterranean cities, made up of mazes of streets, lanes and alleys, where at times one cannot even see the sky because it is covered by rows of awnings that, besides sheltering from the sun, give a sense of protection, refuge and isolation.

Headquarters of Vacheron &Constantin, B. Tschumi, Geneva, 2001-2005.

Research and Multimedia Centre *Grappa Nardini*, Studio Fuksas, Bassano del Grappa, Italy, 2004.

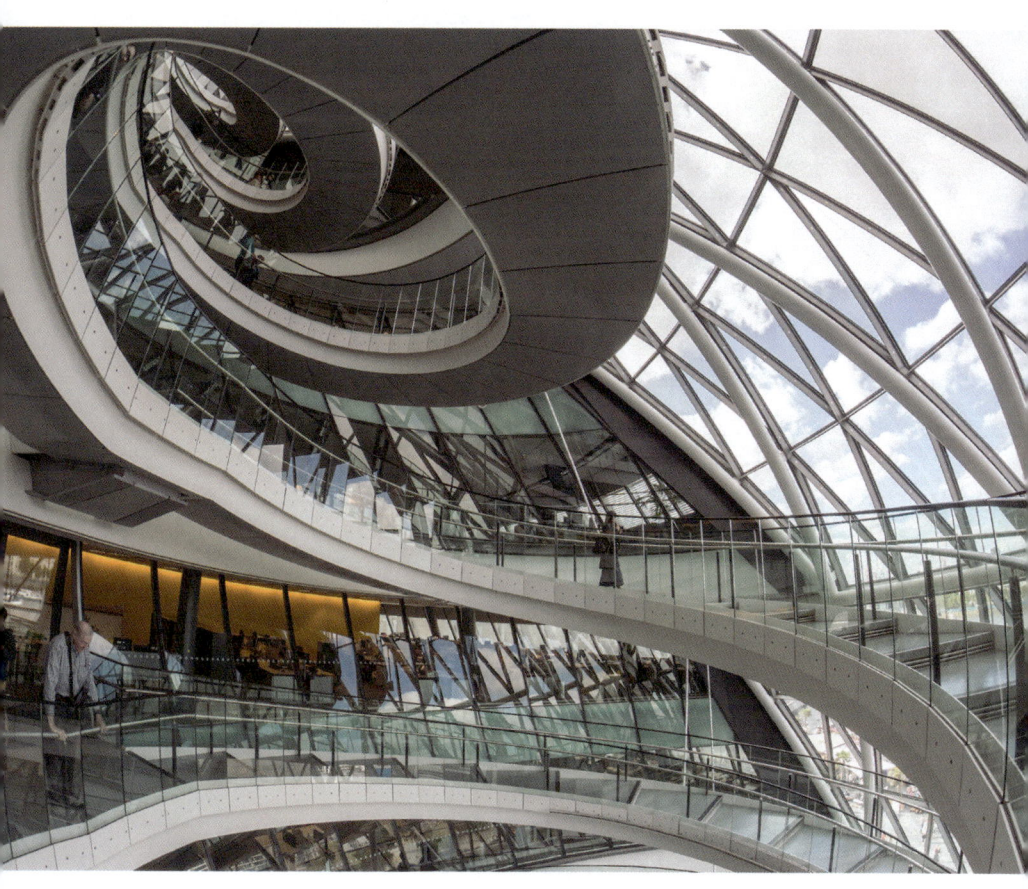

City Hall, N. Foster, London, 1999-2002.

To counterpoise a labyrinthine space, stark elements emerge from the fabric. These may be out-of-scale objects which distinguish themselves by their immense proportions. In the case of semi-underground structures, these elements may be light sources, which by their exceptional nature and the surprise that provoke, are a nodal point that attracts and gives off energy, a kind of fulcrum.

In the new Louvre project in Paris the exceptional points are pyramid-shaped capteurs of light, elements which help to enhance the archaeological finds. The ruins are in fact put on display, illuminated by oblique shafts of light from the ground upwards and become stopoff points that invite the visitor to pause, where he can stop for a contact with the outside world or take in a view of the whole. Generally, these spaces are indicated by names such as: arena, belvedere, balcony view, names that contribute largely to their success. An appropriate name helps one to memorize them and contributes to making them privileged lookout points.

MyZeil Shopping Mall, Studio Fuksas, Frankfurt, 2009.

Silo towers, MVRDV, Copenhagen, 2005.

Interiors of Selfridges Building, Future Systems, Birmingham, Great Britain, 2003.

Palariccione, A. Anselmi, Riccione, Italy, 2008.

...towards a responsible design

Attention to the environment, the use of renewable sources, the search for eco-friendly materials have become central issues in the architectural debate, although all too often they remain a dead letter.

In this context the evolution of architecture places man at the center and his needs. Respecting the environment and improving the quality of life have become inescapable requirements for whoever wishes to design new realities.

Over the past few years factors have intervened that force architecture to take a stand on the issue of sustainability. There is an even more pressing need to abide by the "protocols" global containment of emissions and energy saving that sees in the Kyoto agreement a starting point for ambitious goals.

The challenge to architects is of great interest: integrating technique and architecture by making substantial typological and morphological changes. In this regard even great public places represent a decisive challenge in this direction.

Such a innovative a process requires an experimental phase in which to identify categories, objectives, instruments and actions. How is it possible to meet the requirement of progressive integration between projects and techniques related to sustainability so that architecture, in coming to grips with the problem, can develop the necessary implications in terms of language?

The pervasive impact of anthropic action on the environment seems to imply the need for a carefully planned coordination of interventions in order to avoid altering the equilibrium between nature and technical objects.

The responsible design seems proactive and simplistic in comparison to some of the innovations that have profoundly affected contemporary life. Hence the need to establish a project theory capable of demonstrating how it is possible, in social and environmental terms, to combine the processes of production, use, consumption and satisfaction.

We must give due importance to the bioclimatic and ecological components of the design space, since the transfer of notions and concepts of a particular discipline does not work mechanically but only as a re-elaboration and signification in architectural terms.

Building innovative systems is an important goal for experimenting and exploring new models of collective life based on social support and mixitè, and at the same time able to renew and interpret architectural, technological and management aspects of great machines of collective living.

Masdar City, N. Foster, United Arab Emirates, 2007-2014.

Meydan – Umraniye Retail Complex & Multiplex, FOA Foreign Office Architects, Istanbul, 2007.

Chapter 5

Caravanserrais,
drawings of Frei Otto.

NOTES

1 Purini 1996.
2 Focault 1994.
3 Purini 1996.
4 Even the most interesting musical experiments of recent years are heading towards these new forms of mixture, contamination of different genres, unknown sensations, often borrowed from the most primitive cultures which give more room to forms of emotivity. So-called primitive societies, whether Australian, African or American, assign a central role to mask, vertigo, imitation and ecstasy, or if we prefer, pantomime and ecstasy, ensuring their intensity and consequently also the cohesion of collective life.
5 Interview with Jean Nouvel, in Colafranceschi 1997.
6 Interview with James Wine -Site, in Colafranceschi 1997.
7 Gregotti 1966.
8 Ugo 1991.
9 Manzini 1990, p. 24.

Bibliography

A.A.V.V.,2011, *This is Hybrid*, Vitoria -Gateiz, a+t architecture publishers.

A.A.V.V., 2007, *La civiltà dei superluoghi*, Bologna, Damiani editore.

A.A.V.V., 2003, *«Lotus»*, n.118, Milano, Editoriale Lotus.

A.A.V.V., 1996, *Le centre commercial entre hangar et cathédrale, Mégalopole-art architecture urbanisme*, cahier n. 13, Givors, Institute Art et Ville, Maison du Rhône.

A.A.V.V., 1991, *L'Espace du public. Les compétences du citadin*, Colloque d'Art-et-Senans 8-9-10 novembre 1990, Paris, Plan Urbain D.A.U.-B.R.A, Editions Recherches.

Alberti, L. B., 1450, *De Re aedificatoria*; 1966, Orlandi, G., eds, Milano, Il Polifilo.

Altoon, R. A., FAIA, 1996, *International Shopping Center Architecture*, New York, International Council of Shopping Centers.

Augé, M., 1992, *Non lieux*, Paris, Seuil; trad. it. 1993, *Non luoghi*, Milano, Eleuthera.

Aymonimo A., Mosco V.P., 2006, *Spazi pubblici contemporanei. Architettura a volume zero*, Milano, Skyra.

Bæk Pedersen, P., 1996, *The contest of simultaneities in the urban space*, Barcellona, P2O3 Atti del XIX Congresso UIA Barcelona.

Ballard, J. G., 1995, *Il futuro è morto. Psicogeografia della modernità*, Milano, Mimesis.

Barbieri, G., 1996, *Forme del progetto urbano in Carpenzano O. Lo spazio delle infrastrutture*,Pescara, Sala ed.

Baudrillard, J., 1976, *La società dei consumi*, Bologna, Il Mulino.

Baudrillard, J., 1987, *L'autre par lui même. Habilitation*, Paris, Editions Galilée; trad. it. 1992, *L'altro visto da sé*, Genova, Costa & Nolan.

Baudrillard, J., 1994, *Il sogno della merce*, Milano, Lupetti & Co.

Bédarida, M., 1992, *Le due città. Euro Disney Park a Marne-la-Vallée*, «Lotus International», n. 71.

Benjamin, W., 1955, *Das Kunstwerk im Zeitalter seiner technischen Reproduzierbarkeit*, Frankfurt am Main, Suhrkamp Verlag; trad. it. 1991, *L'opera d'arte nell'epoca della sua riproducibilità tecnica*, Torino, Einaudi.

Benjamin, W., 1955, *Schriften*, Frankfurt am Main, Suhrkamp Verlag; trad. it. 1995, *Angelus Novus*, Torino, Einaudi.

Benjamin, W., 1972, *"Der destructive Character"*, in *Gesammelte Schriften*, Frankfurt am Main, Suhrkamp; trad. it. 1995, *"Il carattere distruttivo"*, in *Il carattere distruttivo. L'orrore del quotidiano*, Milano, Mimesis.

Benjamin, W., 1972, *Gesammelte Schriften*, Frankfurt am Main, Suhrkamp; trad. it. 1986, *Parigi capitale del XIX secolo. Progetti appunti e materiali 1927-1940*, Torino, Einaudi.

Betsky, A., 2002, *Landscapers: building with the Land*, London, Thames & Hudson.

Bettetini, G., 1996, *"La morte, l'acqua, il soggetto. Racconto e costruzione dell'identità personale nel labirinto delle differenze"*, in AA. VV., *Gli immaginari della differenza. La Triennale nella città*, Triennale di Milano XIX Esposizione Identità Differenze, Milano, Electa.

Bilò, M., 1994, *"Interni"*, in Marucci G., eds, *La città bella*, Milano, Edizioni Sapiens.

Bloch, E., 1923; trad. it. 1980, *Spirito dell'Utopia*, Firenze, La Nuova Italia.

Boeri, S., Lanzani A., Marini E., 1993, *Nuovi Spazi senza nome* in *Casabella* n. 597/598.

Bonomi, A., 1996, *Il trionfo della moltitudine. Forme e conflitti della società che viene*, Torino, Bollati Boringhieri.

Bordini, V., 2006, *Architettura dell'inquietudine*, Torino, editore Allemandi & C.

Bordini, V., 1994, *Spazi pubblici per una città possibile*, «PPC», n. 14, Pescara.

Branzi, A., 1995, *Tutto è metropoli*, «Lotus», n. 84.

Branzi, A., 1996, *Il design dopo Dio (e la poetica dei gommini)*, «Domus», n. 787, novembre, p. 58.

Brenner, K. T., a cura, 1990, *Architettura della metropoli. Sei edifici pubblici per Milano*, Milano, Idea Books.

Burdese, J., Engrand, G., Trelcat S., 1996, *Vers une reconception de la pensée urbaine?*, Barcellona, P236 Atti del XIX Congresso UIA Barcelona.

Cacciari, M., 1986, *Metropoli della mente*, «Casabella», n. 523, aprile.

Cantarelli, R., 2006, *Per una fenomenologia architettonica del centro commerciale*, Materia, n. 52, Motta Architettura, pp. 38-47.

Caillois, R., 1967, *Les jeux et les hommes: le pasque et le vertice*, Paris, Editions Gallimard; trad. it. 1995, *I giochi e gli uomini: la maschera e la vertigine*, Milano, Bompiani.

Calvi, E., 1991, *Tempo e progetto. L'architettura come narrazione*, Milano, Guerini studio.

Calvino, I., 1993, *Lezioni Americane. Sei proposte per il prossimo millennio*, Milano, Oscar Mondadori.

Calvino, I.,2012, *Sono nato in America... Interviste 1951-1985*, Milano, Mondadori.

Canevacci, M., 1994, *"La comunicazione urbana"*, in *La città Polifonica: saggio sull'antropologia della comunicazione urbana*, Roma, Seam.

Canevacci, M., 1995, *Sincretismi. Una esplorazione sulle ibridazioni culturali*, Genova, Costa & Nolan.

Chapter 5

Carones. M., 2011, "Funzionalità/ Polifunzionalità" in AR N.55, Milano, Il Sole 24 ore.

Cenzatti, M., Crawford, M., 1993, Spazi pubblici e mondi paralleli, «Casabella», n. 597-598, pp. 34-38.

Cerasi, M.,1979, Lo spazio collettivo della città, Milano, Mazzotta.

Cervellini, F., 1996, La rappresentazione dello spazio pubblico, «Metamorfosi», n. 29-30, L'architettura degli spazi pubblici.

Choay, F., 1965, L'urbanisme. Utopies et réalité, Paris, Seuil; trad. it. 1973, La città. Utopie e realtà, Torino, Einaudi.

Choay, F., 1992, L'orizzonte del posturbano, Milano, Officina.

Colafranceschi, D., 1995, Architettura in superficie. Materiali figure e tecnologie delle nuove facciate urbane, Roma, Gangemi.

Colafranceschi, D., 1997, Sull'involucro in architettura, Roma, Dedalo.

Crawford, M., 1992, "The world in a shopping mall", in M., Sorkin, a cura, Variations on a Theme Park. The New American City and the End of Public Space, New York, Hill and Wang.

Dachevsky, M., 1996, Los contenedores modeladores de la produccion en la cultura global, Barcellona, PO55 Atti del XIX Congresso UIA Barcelona.

Dal Fabbro, A., 1998, "Nuovi fori della città contemporanea", in ArchInt anno 4, n.6, Venezia, Dreossi editore.

Davis, M., 1993, La città di quarzo. Indagine sul futuro di Los Angeles, Roma, Manifestolibri.

de Boer, M., 1993, "Plazas: the new Shopping Malls", in Architectuur in Nederland Jaarboek 1992-1993, Rotterdam, Nai Uitgevers Publishers.

de Boer, M., 1993, "Public Interiors", in AA. VV., Public Interiors, Amsterdam, Arcam.

De Castro Afeche Pimenta, M., 1996, Flexibilité et nouveaux espaces urbains, Barcellona, P2OO Atti del XIX Congresso UIA Barcelona.

De Cesaris, A., 1993, Tendenza all'astrazione e progressiva denaturalizzazione dell'edificio, Roma, Gangemi.

De Cesaris, A., 2002, Terminal Marittimo di Yokohama, «Industria delle costruzioni», n. 367.

De Cesaris, A., 2004, Infrastrutture e paesaggio urbano, Roma, Edilstampa.

De Cesaris, A., 2006, Il progetto del suolo-sottosuolo, Roma, Gangemi.

de Hoog, M., 1993, "The inside of Amsterdam", in AA. VV., Public Interior, Amsterdam, Aarcam.

Dell'Aira, V. P., 2005, Architetture per il commercio, Roma, Edilstampa.

De Parville, H., L'exposition universelle (1889); trad. it. 1890, Parigi e l'Esposizione universale del 1889, Milano, Fratelli Treves.

De Rossi, P., 1996, L'architecture, un art qui fait de la place, Barcellona, DC06 Atti del XIX Congresso UIA Barcelona.

de Solà Morales, I., 1991, Mnemosi o retorica: la crisi della rappresentazione nella città e nell'architettura moderna, «Quaderni di Lotus», Atlante metropolitano, Milano, Electa.

Debord, G., 1988, Commentaire sur la Société du spectacle, Paris, Editions Gérard Lebovici; trad. it. 1990, Commentari sulla società dello spettacolo, Milano, SugarCo.

Desideri, F., 1984, Il vero non ha finestre. Note su ottica e dialettica nel Passagen Werk di Benjamin, Bologna, Cappelli.

Desideri, P., 1995, La città di latta, Genova, Costa & Nolan.

Dethier, J., 1991, Storia e attualità del ponte abitato, «Rassegna», Ponti abitati, n. 48, dicembre.

Dorfles, G., 1979, Artificio e natura, Torino, Einaudi.

Dunlop, B., 1996, Building a dream. The art of Disney Architecture, NewYork, Harry N. Abrams, Inc. Publishers.

Eco, U., 1986, Travels in Hiper-Reality, London, Picador.

Eliseo, M., Piccione, P., 2001, Transatlantici. Storia delle grandi navi passeggeri italiane, Tormena Ed., Genova

Espuche, A. G., 1996, "Containers of Pause", in AA.VV., Present and Future Architecture in Cities, XIX Congresso UIA, Barcellona, UIA Barcelona.

"Euralille- Poser, Exposer", catalogo della mostra, Lille, 1996.

Featherstone, M., 1995, Cultura del consumo e postmodernismo, Roma, edizioni Seam.

Feiler, M., 1985, Going place, London, Macmillan.

Ferlenga, A., a cura, 1989, Aldo Rossi. Architetture 1959-1987, Milano, Electa.

Filarete, 1464, Trattato di architettura, Grassi, L., a cura, 1972, Milano, Il Polifilo.

Foucault, M., 1986, Spazi altri. I principi dell'eterotopia, «Lotus international», n. 48-49, pp. 9-17.

Foucault, M., 1994, Eterotopia. Luoghi e non luoghi metropolitani, Milano, Mimesis.

Frampton, K., 1980, Modern Architecture: a critical History, London, Thames and Hudson; trad. it. 1982, Storia dell'architettura moderna, Bologna, Zanichelli.

Foreign Office Architect, 2002, The Yokohama project, Barcellona, Actar.

Casabella, 2003, n. 708.

Fumo, M., 2005, Dal mercato ambulante all'outlet. Luoghi e

architetture per il commercio, ed. Compositori.

Futagawa, Y., 1996, Jean Nouvel, «GA Document extra», n. 07, Tokyo, A.D.A. EDITA Tokyo.

Geist, J. F., 1973, Passagen. Ein Bautyp des 19 jahrhunderts, München, Prestel-Verlag; trad. fr. 1989, Le passage. Un type architectural du XIXe siècle, Liège-Bruxelles, Pierre Mardaga éditeur.

Glusberg, J., 1996, "Risurrezione del luogo pubblico", in AA. VV., Il padiglione Italia. Paesi e istituzioni, Triennale di Milano XIX Esposizione Identità Differenze, Milano, Electa.

Gregotti, V., 1966, Il territorio dell'architettura, Milano, Feltrinelli.

Gregotti, V., Matteoni, D., 1991, Introduzione, «Rassegna», Ponti abitati, n. 48, dicembre.

Gregotti,V., 2011, "Dello Spazio Pubblico", in Architettura e postmetropoli, Giulio Einaudi ed.

Hall, P., 1988, "Anonimia e identità nella supermetropoli", in L. Mazza, a cura, Le città del mondo e il futuro delle metropoli. Partecipazioni internazionali, XVII Triennale, Milano, Electa, pp. 43-62.

Harvey, D., 1990, The condition of Postmodernity, Basil, Blackwell; trad. it. 1993, La crisi della modernità, Milano, Il Saggiatore.

Harvey, D., 1991, I luoghi urbani all'interno del "villaggio globale". Riflessioni sulla condizione urbana nel capitalismo del tardo Novecento, «Quaderni di Lotus», Atlante metropolitano, Milano, Electa.

Hajer M., Reijndorp A.,2002, In search of the new public domain, Rotterdam, NAi publishers.

Heidegger, M., 1950; trad. it. 1984, "L'origine dell'opera d'arte", in Sentieri interrotti, Firenze, La Nuova Italia.

Heidegger, M., 1954; trad. it. 1980, "La cosa", in Saggi e discorsi, Milano, Mursia.

Hertzberger, H., 1991, Lessons for Students in Architecture, Rotterdam, Uitgeverij 010 Publishers; trad. it. 1996, Lezioni di architettura, Bari, Editori Laterza.

Huizinga, J., 1939, Homo ludens; trad. it. 1973, Homo ludens, Torino, Einaudi.

Iacono, A. M., 1995, Tra individui e cose, Roma, Manifestolibri.

Ilardi M., a cura, 1990, La città senza luoghi. Individuo, conflitto, consumo nella metropoli, Genova, Costa & Nolan.

Ilardi, M., 1995, "Lo spazio pubblico nella città diffusa", in G. Marucci, a cura, Limiti della città. Il borgo, la metropoli, Milano, Sapiens.

Illuminati, A., 1995, La città e i desideri, Roma, Manifestolibri.

Illuminati, A., 1996, La lotta sullo spazio pubblico e sulla cittadinanza nella metropoli moderna, «Metamorfosi», L'architettura degli spazi pubblici, n. 29-30.

Ingersoll, R., 1992, Il centro commerciale Fantasmagoria II, «Casabella», n. 586-587 gennaio-febbraio, pp. 62-69.

Ingersoll, R., 1993, Jumpcut Urbanism, «Casabella», n. 597-598, gennaio-febbraio, pp. 52-57.

Ingersoll, R., 1995, "La fine metafisica della polis", Marucci, G., eds, I limiti della città. Il borgo ela metropoli, Milano, Sapiens.

Ingersoll, R., 1996, L'internazionale del turista, «Casabella», n. 630-631, gennaio-febbraio.

Intorno allo shopping/Shopping environs in Lotus n.118, Milano, 2003.

Jackson, J. B., 1992, Sulla strada in auto o a piedi, «Casabella», n. 586-587, gennaio-febbraio, pp. 14-21.

Jameson, F., 1984, Postmodernism, or the cultural Logic of Late Capitalism, New Left Review;

trad. it. 1989, Il post moderno, o la logica culturale del tardo capitalismo, Milano, Garzanti.

Joseph, I., a cura, 1995, Prendre place. Espace public et culture dramatique, Colloque de Cerisy, Condé-sur-Noireau, Editions Recherches - Plan Urbain.

Kolbowsky, S., 1996, "Something for Nothing", in AA.VV., Present and Future Architecture in Cities, XIX Congresso UIA, Barcellona, UIA Barcelona 96.

Koolhaas, R., 1994, Bigness, ovvero il problema della Grande Dimensione, «Domus» n. 764, ottobre, p. 87.

Koolhaas, R., 1994, Delirious New York, New York, The Monacelli Press.

Koolhaas, R., OMA, Mau, B., 1995, Small, Medium, Large, Extralarge, New York, Monicelli Press.

Koolhaas, R., 2001, Project on the city 2, Köln, Taschen.

Koolhaas, R.,2011, Singapore Songlines, Macerata, Quodlibet.

Lash, S., 1990, Sociology of Postmodernism, London, Routledge.

Le commerce et la ville... in Architecture Interieure n.275, 1997, pp. 32-37.

Liperi, F., 1995, Città sonore. Realtà urbana e produzione musicale, Genova, Costa & Nolan.

Loriers, M. C., 1995, Espace publics couverts: tendances, «Techniques & Architecture», n. 420, giugno-luglio, pp. 70-75.

Loyer, B., 1995, Atrium: nouvelles facettes d'une typologie, «Techniques&Architecture», n. 420, giugno-luglio.

Lucan, J., 1990, Oma. Rem Koolhaas. Architetture 1970-1990, Milano, Electa.

Lucan, J., 1993, Lo spazio urbano nell'era dell'individualismo, «Casabella», n. 597-598, gennaio-febbraio, pp. 77-79.

Chapter 5

Lyotard, J. F., 1979, *La condition postmoderne*, Paris, Les editions de Minuit; trad. it. 1993, *La condizione postmoderna*, Milano, Feltrinelli, p. 5.

Macci, L., Casalini, I., Comodini, M., 1990, *Centri multifunzionali in Europa*, Firenze, Alinea.

Manzini, E., 1990, *Artefatti. Verso una nuova ecologia dell'ambiente artificiale*, Milano, Domus Academy.

Marrey, B., 1979, *Les grand magasins*, Paris, Picard.

Marti Aris, C., 1990, *Le variazioni dell'identità. Il tipo in architettura*, Milano, Clup.

Mauger, P., 1991, *Centres commerciaux*, Paris, Editions du Moniteur; trad. it., 1993, *Centri commerciali*, Milano, Tecniche nuove.

Mc Kean, J., 1994, *Crystal Palace*, London, Phaidon Press.

Mertins, D., 1988, "Trasformazioni metropolitane: l'architettura degli spazi pubblici emergenti", in L. Mazza, a cura, *Le città del mondo e il futuro delle metropoli. Partecipazioni internazionali*, XVII Triennale, Milano, Electa.

Metamorfosi, 1996, *L'architettura degli spazi pubblici*, n. 29-30.

Moore, C., 1965, *You have to Pay for the Public Life*, «Perspecta», n. 9/10.

Morandi, M., 1996, *La città vissuta. Significati e valori dello spazio urbano*, Firenze, Alinea.

8. Mostra Internazionale di Architettura, 2002, Next, La Biennale di Venezia, Venezia, Marsilio.

Nicolin, P., 1996, "The Fourth Typology", in AA.VV., *Present and Future Architecture in Cities*, XIX Congresso UIA, Barcellona, UIA Barcelona.

Norberg-Schulz, C., 1979, *Genius loci. Towards a Phenomenology of Architecture*, New York, Rizzoli International Publications; trad. it. 1998, *Genius loci: paesaggio, ambiente, architettura*, Milano, Electa.

Panella, R., a cura, 1997, *Piazze e nuovi luoghi collettivi di Roma*, Roma, Fratelli Palombi Editori.

Pavia R., 1996, *Identità dei luoghi e progetto urbano in Carpenzano O. Lo spazio delle infrastrutture*, Pescara, Sala ed.

Pazzaglini, M., 1993, *Architettura: logos e racconto. Elementi per una teoria del progetto*, Roma, Kappa.

Perniola, M., 1990, *Enigmi. Il momento egizio nella società e nell'arte*, Genova, Costa & Nolan.

Perniola, M., 1995, *Oltre il desiderio e il piacere. Territori dell'estremo e spaesamento*, Milano, Mimesis,

Perniola, M., a cura, 1994, *L'aria si fa tesa. Per una filosofia del sentire*, Genova, Costa & Nolan.

Petruccioli, A.,1985, *Dar al Islam*, Roma, Carucci.

Petrilli, A., 1995, *Crystal Palace*, «Spazio e Società», n. 69, pp. 126-128.

Piano, R., 1986, *Dialoghi di cantiere*, Bari, Laterza.

Piano, R., 1995, in «GB Progetti osservatorio internazionale», n. 39, settembre.

Pollok,S.,2006, "Un guscio prezioso" e "Un sipario urbano", in L'Architetto, n.16, Roma, Mancosu editore.

Portoghesi P., 2006, *Le nuove forme del mercato*, Materia n. 52, Motta Architettura, pp. 24-27

Pousse, J. F., 1995, *Passages: le renouveau*, «Techniques & Architecture»", n. 420, giugno-luglio, pp. 50-54.

Prestinenza Puglisi, L., 1996, *Rem Koolhaas. Trasparenze metropolitane*, Roma, testo & immagine.

Proust, M., 1927, *À la recherche du temps perdu*, Paris, Editions Gallimard; trad. it. 1954, *Alla ricerca del tempo perduto*, Torino, Einaudi.

Purini, F., 1992, *Altre congetture*, «Edilizia Popolare», n. 219.

Purini, F., 1996, *Il linguaggio architettonico come spazio pubblico dell'architettura*, «Metamorfosi. Quaderni di Architettura», n. 29 / 30.

Rassegna, 1991, *Ponti abitati*, n. 48, dicembre.

Rella, F., 1982, introduzione a Aragon, L., *Il paesano di Parigi*, Milano, Il Saggiatore.

Rella, F., 1984, *Metamorfosi, Immagini del pensiero*, Milano, Feltrinelli.

Ricoeur, P., 1983, *Temps et Récite*, Paris, Seuil.

Ricoeur, P., 1995, "Architettura e narratività", in AA. VV., *Gli immaginari della differenza. La Triennale nella città*, Triennale di Milano XIX Esposizione Identità Differenze, Milano, Electa.

Rocca, A., 1996, "Disparition et réapparition des lieux", in AA.VV., *Le centre commercial entre hangar et cathédrale, Mégalopole-art architecture5urbanisme*, cahier n. 13, Givors, Institute Art et Ville, Maison du Rhône.

Rosenkranz, K., 1994, *L'estetica del brutto*, Milano, Edizioni Olivares.

Rossi, P., a cura, 1954, *Critica della ragione storica*, Torino, Einaudi.

Rossi, P.O., 2012, *Guida all'architettura moderna 1909-2011*, Roma-Bari, Laterza.

Rossi, P.O., 1996, *La costruzione del progetto architettonico*, Roma-Bari, Laterza.

Rowe, C., Koetter, F., 1979, *Collage city*, Cambridge, Mass.; trad. it. 1981, *Collage city*, Milano, Il Saggiatore.

Rustin, M., 1991, *Per chi sono gli spazi pubblici?*, «Quaderni di Lotus», Atlante metropolitano, Milano, Electa.

Rykwert, J., 1972, *On Adam's House in Paradise*; trad. it. 1972, *La casa di Adamo in Paradiso*, Milano, Adelphi.

Sanchez Mèrina, F. J., 1996, "The future always looks good" in the golden land, Barcellona, PO66 Atti del XIX Congresso UIA Barcelona 96.

Saxon, R., 1993, *The atrium comes of age*, Harlow Essex, Longman Group.

Secchi, B., 1993, *Un'urbanistica di spazi aperti*, «Casabella», n. 597-598, pp. 77-79.

Secchi, R., 1991, "Centri commerciali. La simulazione dell'urbano", in *L'architettura degli spazi commerciali*, Roma, Officina edizioni.

Sennet, R., 1977, *The Fall of Public Man*, New York, A. Knopf; trad. it. 1982, *Il declino dell'uomo pubblico: la società intimista*, Milano, Bompiani.

Sennet, R., 1988, *Palais Royal*, Milano, Feltrinelli.

Sennet, R., 1990, *The coscience of the eye. The design and social life of cities*, New York, A. Knopf; trad. it. 1992, *La coscienza dell'occhio. Progetto e vita sociale nelle città*, Milano, Feltrinelli.

Seppilli, A., 1977, *Sacralità dell'acqua e sacrilegio dei ponti*, Palermo, Sellerio.

Shopping Malls, *Architectural Design*, Edizione Structure, Barcellona, 2005.

Simmel, G., 1909, *Der Tag*, 15, IX; trad. it. 1970, *Saggi di estetica*, Padova, Liviana Editrice.

Sims, E.,1978, "Markets and Caravanserrais", in *Architecture of the Islamic world*, London, Thames & Hudson Ltd.

Sinnott, E. W., 1963, *The problem of Organic Form*, New Haven, Yale University Press.

Sorkin, M., 1996 "Container Riff", in AA.VV., *Present and Future Architecture in Cities*, XIX Congresso UIA, Barcellona, UIA Barcelona.

Steiner, D., 1996, *A Diary of Disney's Celebration*, «Domus», n. 787, novembre, pp. 43-48.

Struijs, M., 1996, *The mirror of the sublime*, Barcellona, P211 Atti del XIX Congresso UIA Barcelona 96.

Tafuri, M., 1980, *La sfera e il labirinto. Avanguardie e architettura da Piranesi agli anni 70*, Torino, Einaudi.

Terranova, A., 1996, *Passaggi in paesaggi di passeggio*, «Metamorfosi», n. 29-30.

Teyssot, G., 1991, *Il "teatro" della metropoli: conclusioni e interrogativi*, «Quaderni di Lotus», Atlante metropolitano, Milano, Electa.

Thermes, L., 1995, "Lo spazio abitativo come entità metamorfica, il terziario come modello della residenza", in G. Marucci, a cura, *I limiti della città. Il borgo e la metropoli*, Milano, Sapiens.

Torricelli, G. P., 2009,*Potere e spazio pubblico urbano. Dall'agorà alla baraccopoli*, Loreto, Academia Universa Press.

Tosetto, D., 1986, *Parchi ricreativi nel mondo*, Padova, Facto Edizioni.

Tschumi, B., 1994, *Event-Cities*, Cambridge, Massachusetts/London, England, The Mit Press.

Tschumi B., 2005, *Architettura e disgiunzione*, Bologna, Pendragon.

Turchini,G., 2011, "Multifunzionalità come strumento di integrazione" in AR N.55, Milano, Il Sole 24 ore.

Ugo, V., 1981, "L'architettura a dismisura d'uomo", in AA. VV., *L'espressionismo*, Roma, Newton Compton.

Ugo, V., 1991, *I luoghi di Dedalo. Elementi teorici dell'architettura*, Bari, Dedalo.

Urry, J., 1995, *Lo sguardo del turista. Il tempo libero e il viaggio nelle società contemporanee*, Roma, Seam.

Van Eyck, A., 1962, *Lament for Stockholm*, «Architectural Design», 12, vol. XXXII, p. 602.

Vattimo, G., 1989, *La società trasparente*, Milano, Garzanti.

Venturi, R., 1966, *Complexity and contradiction in architecture*, New York, The Museum of Modern Art; trad. it. 1982, *Complessità e contraddizione in architettura*, Bari, Dedalo.

Venturi, R., Scott Brown, D., 1996, *Las Vegas postclassica*, «Domus», n. 787, novembre, pp. 9-10.

Venturi, R., Scott Brown, D., Izenour, S., 1985, *Imparando da Las Vegas*, Venezia, Cluva Editrice.

Vercelloni, M., 1996, *I parchi a tema Disney*, «Domus», n. 787, novembre, pp. 35-39.

Villani, T., 1994, "Il simulacro occidentale. Conflitti e modernità", in P. Virilio, *La deriva dei continenti*, Milano, Mimesis.

Virilio, P., 1984, *L'espace critique*, Christian Bourgois Editeur; trad. it. 1988, *Lo spazio critico*, Bari, Edizioni Dedalo.

Virilio, P., 1989, *Estètique de la disparition*, Paris, Editions Galilée; trad. it. 1992, *Estetica della sparizione*, Napoli, Liguori Editore.

Visentin, C., 2006, *La seduzione del luogo. Cronistorie e futuro dello shopping mall*, Materia, n. 52, Motta Architettura, pp. 30-37.

von Moos, S., 1996, *La "sindrome di Disney"*, «Domus», n. 787, novembre, pp. 4-5.

Zardini, M., 1994, *Pelle, muro, facciata*, «Lotus», n. 82, pp. 39-55.

Zardini, M., 1996, "Tout sous un même toit. Trente ans plus tard", in AA.VV., *Le centre commercial entre hangar et cathédrale*, Mégalopole-art architecture urbanisme, cahier n. 13, Givors, Institute Art et Ville, Maison du Rhône.

Zecchi, S., 1996, *Il brutto e il bello*, Milano, Mondatori.

Chapter 5

Image sources

AA. VV., *Le arti di Piranesi*, 2009 Marsilio editore.

Accorsi, F., *Lettere e lustrini*, "Europ'A", n. 8, primavera/estate 2009, pp. 44-47.

Betsky, A., 2002, *Landscrapers: building with the Land*, London, Thames & Hudson.

Bucci, F., California Academy of sciences, "il richiamo della foresta", "Casabella", n.791, luglio 2010, pp. 82-97.

Centro Congressi di Herzog e de Meuron in *Domus*, gennaio 2004, pp. 43-45,

Clozza, M., Emergenza Eclettica, <<Europ'A>>, n. 11, primavera/estate 2009, pp. 40-43.

Colafranceschi, D., 1995, *Architettura in superficie. Materiali figure e tecnologie delle nuove facciate urbane*, Roma, Gangemi.

Colafranceschi, D., 1997, *Sull'involucro in architettura*, Roma, Dedalo.

Crawford, M., 1992, "The world in a shopping mall", in M., Sorkin, a cura, *Variations on a Theme Park. The New American City and the End of Public Space*, New York, Hill and Wang.

Dachevsky, M., 1996, *Los contenedores modeladores de la produccion en la cultura global*, Barcellona, PO55 Atti del XIX Congresso UIA Barcelona.

de Boer, M., 1993, "Plazas: the new Shopping Malls", in *Architectuur in Nederland Jaarboek 1992-1993*, Rotterdam, Nai Uitgevers Publishers.

de Boer, M., 1993, "Public Interiors", in AA. VV., *Public Interiors*, Amsterdam, Arcam.

Casabella, 2003, n. 708.

De Castro Afeche Pimenta, M., 1996, *Flexibilité et nouveaux espaces urbains*, Barcellona, P2OO Atti del XIX Congresso UIA Barcelona.

De Cesaris, A., 2004, *Infrastrutture e paesaggio urbano*, Roma, Edilstampa.

de Hoog, M., 1993, "The inside of Amsterdam", in AA. VV., *Public Interior*, Amsterdam, Arcam.

De Parville, H., *L'exposition universelle (1889)*; trad. it. 1890, *Parigi e l'Esposizione universale del 1889*, Milano, Fratelli Treves.

De Rossi, P., 1996, *L'architecture, un art qui fait de la place*, Barcellona, DC06 Atti del XIX Congresso UIA Barcelona.

de Solà Morales, I., 1991, *Mnemosi o retorica: la crisi della rappresentazione nella città e nell'architettura moderna*, <<Quaderni di Lotus>>, Atlante metropolitano, Milano, Electa.

Desideri, F., 1984, *Il vero non ha finestre. Note su ottica e dialettica nel Passagen Werk di Benjamin*, Bologna, Cappelli.

Dethier, J., 1991, *Storia e attualità del ponte abitato*, Rassegna, *Ponti abitati*, n. 48, dicembre.

Dragon promenade in Architectural. Review n°10 dic. 1998.

Dunlop, B., 1996, *Building a dream. The art of Disney Architecture*, NewYork, Harry N. Abrams, Inc. Publishers.

EL Croquis n°123, Toyo Ito 2001-2005, maggio 2004 pp. 50-51.

Espuche, A. G., 1996, "Containers of Pause", in AA.VV., *Present and Future Architecture in Cities*, XIX Congresso UIA, Barcellona, UIA Barcelona.

Feiler, M., 1985, *Going place*, London, Macmillan.

Filarete, 1464, *Trattato di architettura*, Grassi, L., a cura, 1972, Milano, Il Polifilo.

Foreign Office Architect, 2002, *The Yokoama project*, Barcellona, Actar.

Frampton, K., 1980, *Modern Architecture: a critical History*, London, Thames and Hudson; trad.

it. 1982, *Storia dell'architettura moderna*, Bologna, Zanichelli.

Futagawa, Y., 1996, Jean Nouvel, <<GA Document extra>>, n. 07, Tokyo, A.D.A. EDITA Tokyo.

Geist, J. F., 1973, *Passagen. Ein Bautyp des 19 jahrhunderts*, München, Prestel-Verlag; trad. fr. 1989, *Le passage. Un type architectural du XIXe siècle*, Liège-Bruxelles, Pierre Mardaga éditeur.

Glusberg, J., 1996, "Risurrezione del luogo pubblico", in AA. VV., Il padiglione Italia. Paesi e istituzioni, Triennale di Milano XIX Esposizione Identità Differenze, Milano, Electa.

Gregotti, V., Matteoni, D., 1991, Introduzione, Rassegna, Ponti abitati, n. 48, dicembre.

Harvey, D., 1991, *I luoghi urbani all'interno del "villaggio globale". Riflessioni sulla condizione urbana nel capitalismo del tardo Novecento*, Quaderni di Lotus, Atlante metropolitano, Milano, Electa.

Heidegger, M., 1950; trad. it. 1984, "L'origine dell'opera d'arte", in *Sentieri interrotti*, Firenze, La Nuova Italia.

Heidegger, M., 1954; trad. it. 1980, "La cosa", in *Saggi e discorsi*, Milano, Mursia.

Hertzberger, H., 1991, *Lessons for Students in Architecture*, Rotterdam, Uitgeverij 010 Publishers; trad. it. 1996, *Lezioni di architettura*, Bari, Editori Laterza.

Huizinga, J., 1939, *Homo ludens*; trad. it. 1973, *Homo ludens*, Torino, Einaudi.

Iacono, A. M., 1995, *Tra individui e cose*, Roma, Manifestolibri.

Joseph, I., a cura, 1995, *Prendre place. Espace public et culture dramatique*, Colloque de Cerisy, Condé-sur-Noireau, Editions Recherches - Plan Urbain.

Kolbowsky, S., 1996, "Something for Nothing", in AA.VV., *Present and Future Architecture in Cities*, XIX Congresso UIA, Barcellona, UIA Barcelona.

Koolhaas, R., 1994, *Delirious New York*, New York, The Monacelli Press.

Koolhaas, R., OMA, Mau, B., 1995, *Small, Medium, Large, Extralarge*, New York, Monicelli Press.

Koolhas, R., *Harvard design school guide to shopping*, Taschen, 2001 p. 343.

Lamarre, F., *Sotto la volta del CNIT*, "Europ'A", n. 11, primavera/estate 2009, pp. 58-61.

Loriers, M. C., 1995, *Espace publics couverts: tendances*, « Techniques & Architecture », n. 420, giugno-luglio, pp. 70-75.

Loyer, B., 1995, *Atrium: nouvelles facettes d'une typologie*, Techniques&Architecture, n. 420, giugno-luglio.

Lucan, J., 1990, *Oma. Rem Koolhaas. Architetture 1970-1990*, Milano, Electa.

Macci, L., Casalini, I., Comodini, M., 1990, *Centri multifunzionali in Europa*, Firenze, Alinea.

Marrey, B., 1979, *Les grand magasins*, Paris, Picard.

Mauger, P., 1991, *Centres commerciaux*, Paris, Editions du Moniteur; trad. it., 1993, *Centri commerciali*, Milano, Tecniche nuove.

Mc Kean, J., 1994, *Crystal Palace*, London, Phaidon Press.

Mertins, D., 1988, "*Trasformazioni metropolitane: l'architettura degli spazi pubblici emergenti*", in L. Mazza, a cura, *Le città del mondo e il futuro delle metropoli. Partecipazioni internazionali, XVII Triennale*, Milano, Electa.

Nicolin, P., 1996, "*The Fourth Typology*", in AA.VV., *Present and Future Architecture in Cities*, XIX Congresso UIA, Barcellona, UIA Barcelona.

Norberg-Schulz, C., 1979, *Genius loci. Towards a Phenomenology of Architecture*, New York, Rizzoli International Publications; trad. it. 1998, *Genius loci: paesaggio, ambiente, architettura*, Milano, Electa.

Petrilli, A., 1995, *Crystal Palace*, <<Spazio e Società>>, n. 69, pp. 126-128.

Piano, R., 1986, *Dialoghi di cantiere*, Bari, Laterza.

Piano, R., 1995, in <<GB Progetti osservatorio internazionale>>, n. 39, settembre.

Piscitelli, V., 2009, *Riprogettare dopo il sisma*, <<Europ'A>>, n. 12, inverno 2009, pp. 46-49.

Plaroy edificio Forum in Arquitectura Viva n. 84, maggio giugno 2002, p. 3.

Pousse, J. F., 1995, *Passages: le renouveau*, <<Techniques & Architecture>>,n. 420, giugno-luglio, pp. 50-54.

Prestinenza Puglisi, L., 1996, *Rem Koolhaas*.

Trasparenze metropolitane, Roma, testo & immagine.

Rassegna, 1991, Ponti abitati, n. 48, dicembre.

Rassegna n° 4 anno 1991 pag. 60, ponte vecchio a Firenze.

Della Badia, L., - Rizzo, L., *Distillate trasparenze*, <<Europ'A>>, n. 8, primavera/estate 2009, pp. 28-31.

Rocca, A., 1996, "*Disparition et réapparition des lieux*", in AA.VV., *Le centre commercial entre hangar et cathédrale, Mégalopole-art architecture urbanisme*, cahier n. 13, Givors, Institute Art et Ville, Maison du Rhône.

Rustin, M., 1991, *Per chi sono gli spazi pubblici?*, <<Quaderni di Lotus>>, Atlante metropolitano, Milano, Electa.

Rykwert, J., 1972, *On Adam's House in Paradise*; trad. it. 1972, *La casa di Adamo in Paradiso*, Milano, Adelphi.

Saxon, R., 1993, *The atrium comes of age*, Harlow Essex, Longman Group.

Secchi, R.,1991, *L'Architettura degli spazi commerciali*, officina edizioni, Roma, p. 113.

Sorkin, M., 1996 "*Container Riff*", in AA.VV., *Present and Future Architecture in Cities*, XIX Congresso UIA, Barcellona, UIA Barcelona.

Steiner, D., 1996, *A Diary of Disney's Celebration*, Domus, n. 787, novembre, pp. 43-48.

Struijs, M., 1996, *The mirror of the sublime*, Barcellona, P211 Atti del XIX Congresso UIA Barcelona.

Tosetto, D., 1986, *Parchi ricreativi nel mondo*, Padova, Facto Edizioni.

Tschumi, B., 1994, *Event-Cities*, Cambridge, Massachusetts/ London, England, The Mit Press.

Ugo, V., 1991, *I luoghi di Dedalo. Elementi teorici dell'architettura*, Bari, Dedalo.

Van Eyck, A., 1962, *Lament for Stockholm*, <<Architectural Design>>, 12, vol. XXXII, p. 602.

Vercelloni, M., 1996, *I parchi a tema Disney*, <<Domus>>, n. 787, novembre, pp. 35-39.

von Moos, S., 1996, *La "sindrome di Disney"*, <<Domus>>, n. 787, novembre, pp. 4-5.

Zardini, M., 1996, "*Tout sous un même toit. Trente ans plus tard*", in AA.VV., *Le centre commercial entre hangar et cathédrale, Mégalopole-art architecture urbanisme*, cahier n. 13, Givors, Institute Art et Ville, Maison du Rhône.

Zecchi, S., 1996, *Il brutto e il bello*, Milano, Mondatori.

Yearbook 2004 n°5.

Photographs

Mario Ferrari: Cap.3 p.96;

Roberto Grio: Cap.1 p.18; Cap.4 p.119; 136-137; Cap.5 p.197; p.199; p.214;

Jacob+MacFarlane – N.Borel: Cap. 4 p.121; Cap. 5 p.189;

Duccio Malagamba: Cap.4 p.162;

Dea Politano: Cap.1 p.21, Cap.5 p.117; Cap. 5 p.195;

Erminia Sciacchitano: Cap. 1 p.30;

Biljana Stevanovska: Cap.4 p.179; Cap.5 p.213;

of the author Cap. 1 p.114; Cap.4 p.170.

Chapter 5

Acknowledgements

My heartfelt thanks to all those who, at different times and in various ways, lent their support for this book.
To Mario Ferrari and Lucia Ferroglio who worked for the coordination and review of the book.
To Giulia Giampiccolo, Elena Immè who worked with care, passion and dedication on editing and image processing.
To Mimosa Bolatti Guzzo who constantly supervised the graphic design.
A special thanks to Giovanna Lo Re and Emma Tagliacollo who patiently edited and revised all texts.

CONTEMPORARY CARAVANSERRAIS
New models for public spaces and city squares

Author
Guendalina Salimei

Published by
LISt Lab
info@listlab.eu
www.listlab.eu

Editorial Director LISt Lab
Alessandro Martinelli

Art Director & Production
Blacklist Creative, BCN
blacklist-creative.com

Translation
Edward Tosques

ISBN 9788895623412

**Printed and bound
in the European Union**
July 2019 (first edition)

All rights reserved
© of the edition LISt Lab
© of the text the authors
© of the images the authors

Series **BABEL**

No part of this book may be reproduced, stored in a retrieval system, or transmitted in any form or by any means, including electronic, mechanical, photocopying, microfilming, recording or otherwise without written permission from the publisher.

Sales, Marketing and Distribution
distribution@listlab.eu
www.listlab.eu/en/distribuzione/

For more information concerning LIStLab's Scientific Boards please visit the webpage:
www.listlab.eu/en/boards/

LIStLab is an editorial workshop, based in Europe, that works on contemporary issues. LIStLab not only publishes, but also researches, proposes, promotes, produces, creates networks.

LIStLab is a green company committed to respect the environment. Paper, ink, glues and all processings come from short supply chains and aim at limiting pollution. The print run of books and magazines is based on consumption patterns, thus preventing waste of paper and surpluses. LIStLab aims at the responsibility of the authors and markets, towards the knowledge of a new publishing culture based on resource management.